Spencer,
May the Lord reveal Himself through my words, and may healing & transformation prevail!

Love in Christ,
Mekel ♡

RELAXING INTO THE PAIN

My Journey Into Grief & Beyond

Mekel S. Harris, Ph.D.

Copyright © 2016 Mekel S. Harris, Ph.D.

All rights reserved. No part of this book may be used or reproduced by any means, graphic, electronic, or mechanical, including photocopying, recording, taping or by any information storage retrieval system without the written permission of the author except in the case of brief quotations embodied in critical articles and reviews.

WestBow Press books may be ordered through booksellers or by contacting:

WestBow Press
A Division of Thomas Nelson & Zondervan
1663 Liberty Drive
Bloomington, IN 47403
www.westbowpress.com
1 (866) 928-1240

Because of the dynamic nature of the Internet, any web addresses or links contained in this book may have changed since publication and may no longer be valid. The views expressed in this work are solely those of the author and do not necessarily reflect the views of the publisher, and the publisher hereby disclaims any responsibility for them.

Any people depicted in stock imagery provided by Thinkstock are models, and such images are being used for illustrative purposes only. Certain stock imagery © Thinkstock.

ISBN: 978-1-5127-4707-2 (sc)
ISBN: 978-1-5127-4708-9 (hc)
ISBN: 978-1-5127-4706-5 (e)

Library of Congress Control Number: 2016910322

Print information available on the last page.

WestBow Press rev. date: 6/29/2016

Scripture taken from the Contemporary English Version © 1991, 1992, 1995 by American Bible Society, Used by Permission.

Scripture taken from the Holy Bible, NEW INTERNATIONAL VERSION®. Copyright © 1973, 1978, 1984, 2011 by Biblica, Inc. All rights reserved worldwide. Used by permission. NEW INTERNATIONAL VERSION® and NIV® are registered trademarks of Biblica, Inc. Use of either trademark for the offering of goods or services requires the prior written consent of Biblica US, Inc.

Scripture quotations are from The Holy Bible, English Standard Version® (ESV®), copyright © 2001 by Crossway, a publishing ministry of Good News Publishers. Used by permission. All rights reserved.

All Scripture quotations in this publications are from The Message. Copyright © by Eugene H. Peterson 1993, 1994, 1995, 1996, 2000, 2001, 2002. Used by permission of NavPress Publishing Group.

Scripture taken from The Living Bible copyright © 1971 by Tyndale House Foundation. Used by permission of Tyndale House Publishers Inc., Carol Stream, Illinois 60188. All rights reserved. The Living Bible, TLB, and the The Living Bible logo are registered trademarks of Tyndale House Publishers.

Scripture quotations taken from the Holy Bible, New Living Translation, Copyright © 1996, 2004. Used by permission of Tyndale House Publishers, Inc., Wheaton, Illinois 60189. All rights reserved.

Scripture quotations taken from the New American Standard Bible®, Copyright © 1960, 1962, 1963, 1968, 1971, 1972, 1973, 1975, 1977, 1995 by The Lockman Foundation. Used by permission. (www.Lockman.org)

Scripture is taken from GOD'S WORD®, © 1995 God's Word to the Nations. Used by permission of Baker Publishing Group.

CONTENTS

Foreword xv

Introduction xvii

Part 1 : Sometimes, Your Worst Nightmare Becomes Reality!..1

Part 2 : Whatever You Do, Don't Hold Your Breath! 37

Part 3 : New Wineskins and Old Wine!................................ 69

Part 4 : So This Is What Rock Bottom Feels Like!................ 103

Part 5 : Keep Walking into the Fire! 151

Additional Reflections.. 179

Final Thoughts and Prayer 187

To my mother, *Patricia Anne Harris*, a quiet soul who entered this life on June 7, 1949, and exited stage left early in the morning on December 9, 2012. Throughout the thirty-seven years that I was blessed with your presence and wisdom, you always encouraged me to explore new territories and never put limits on my abilities. You were always the captain of my cheering squad, the wind beneath my wings. And even in your physical absence, you continue to inspire me to reach farther than I ever thought possible. I would not have had the courage to take this enormous leap of faith, had it not been for your love, patience, and never-ceasing reassurance. Thank you, Mama. I miss you, and I will always love and long for you! Yet, I know you are with the Father, experiencing the inexplicable joy, peace, and rest you so deserve!

Daddy, thank you for answering the telephone on one of the most devastating days of my life. And thank you for continuing to listen to me cry in the wee hours of the night for weeks. Your support in the months leading up to Mama's death meant so much, and your love in the years following her death has healed so much hurt. I love you with all my heart!

Stanley, your unobtrusive support was invaluable throughout the writing process. Thank you for allowing me to share this journey, of which you are a major part. I pray that my words resonate with you and reflect our beautiful mother in the most honorable and uplifting way. I love the way we have grown together! Mama would be so proud!

Ashley, where do I begin? You have literally seen the best and worst of me, and you still love me! When I think of unconditional support, I think of you. The way you love and care for me is impeccable, and I thank God that He allowed you to cross my path. You will always be my love bug!

Regan, you played a major part in the development of this book—you, your pen, and the way you inspired me to chronicle my thoughts. I am incredibly thankful that God allowed me to cross paths with you at just the right time, in a place where my heart was wide open. Thank you for your gentle kindness!

Amy, you are a major reason that this book came to fruition. When I first sat down in your office, I knew that our therapeutic relationship would pave the way for me to journey through the grief process. Early on, you challenged me to consider what it would be like to "relax into the pain" of my mother's death. I cannot thank you enough for pouring so much of your time, expertise, and genuineness into my broken life and shattered heart. I pray that God continues to use you mightily to serve others and impact their lives in marvelous ways. Should they only experience a measure of what I have experienced, I know their lives will be richly blessed!

Close friends, while not individually named, each of you has played a role in the development of this book. Thank you for not being afraid to journey alongside me over the past three years and supporting me in varying and meaningful ways!

And Jesus Christ, my God, my Rock, mere words will *never* fully characterize all that You are to me. Through sadness, anger, frustration, and sheer pain, You have carried me. Had it not been for Your grace and manifestation at key points along this journey, I know that I would not have had the strength to write this book. I call You, Abba (Father), for You planted the seed for this book throughout the months following my mother's death. You provided opportunities for me to grow the seed through daily journaling. And now, You have helped me water this tree of life, a tree that I pray blesses many who are experiencing their own unique journeys with grief. I love You more than words can say! Thank You for trusting me with this race! I pray that I continue to run it with grace, endurance, and never-ceasing focus on Your goodness!

It is sorrow that opens up within us the capacities of the heavenly life, and it is sorrow that makes us willing to launch our capacities on a boundless sea of service for God and our fellows.

—Anonymous

FOREWORD

Research in the area of grief and loss, particularly research prior to the twenty-first century, highlights the "stages of grief" as if they progress in a linear fashion. If this was, in fact, the case, I can honestly say that my grief experience was *far* from typical! Truth be told, contemporary grief researchers now note that the grief process does not occur in a universal or linear fashion. Rather, it is highly individual, more often cyclical, and typically unpredictable.

As you read my story, you will notice an array of emotional, physical, and spiritual experiences. I encourage you to accept my story as *my* story and consider *your* journey of grief against its own unique backdrop. *After all, each journey deserves its own space.*

INTRODUCTION

Admittedly, I am not a professional writer by trade or experience. My training rests within the field of psychology, specifically with individuals facing disabilities and/or physical illnesses, as well as their families. Yet, I must admit that the totality of all of my professional and personal experiences led me to this place, this "writing space." As a lifelong journal writer, I have always recognized the need within me to tell my story, express my thoughts, and reflect upon my daily experiences as a way of better understanding myself and the situations I have encountered in life. And I have enjoyed experiencing those lightbulb moments across my lifetime, moments when the threads of my life connect in a recognizable way or intersect with new areas that I hope to explore. This book—this adventure really—reflects one of those intersections in my life. Throughout the next several pages, I hope to talk about some of the key intersections that led me to, are presently leading me through, and will hopefully lead me beyond the borders of my mind and spirit. I openly admit that my journey, as well as the language used to describe it in some of my journal entries, is raw at times throughout the book. I pray that you take no offense to the occasional missteps, but that you immerse yourself in the totality of my experience in light of them.

Thank you for allowing me the privilege to share my story, one that may resonate with you as well. It is an ordinary story, though I pray it will inspire extraordinary hope. Blessings to you!

No two persons experience grief in the same way. Rather, God affords each one of us a unique journey, specifically fitted to reveal Himself and allow us deeper understandings of ourselves and the world around us. As I worked toward completion of this book, I realized that my grief path naturally progressed into five parts throughout the course of an (almost) three-year time frame.

PART 1

Sometimes, Your Worst Nightmare Becomes Reality!

Mekel S. Harris, Ph.D.

November 10, 2012

Well, today has been a day like no other in my life! What started off as a typical Saturday morning turned into a day of utter disbelief and heartache. After leaving choir rehearsal this morning, my cell phone rang, and on the other end of the line, I heard Mama's shaky voice. I knew this was unlike her, so I listened intently rather than asking loads of questions or carrying on with usual drama. With wavering in her voice, Mama shared that she received a diagnosis of pancreatic cancer (with metastasis to her lungs and abdomen) only a few minutes prior to the call. Stage IV pancreatic cancer! She had been admitted to the hospital on November 3, 2012, for what Stanley and I thought was another stroke or Crohn's disease flare-up (related to previous medical issues). I recalled that in October, Mama started complaining that she'd lost her appetite and was having trouble tasting her food. No one even considered the possibility of cancer! Mama wept today for less than a minute, and then she said she was ready for "whatever."

At first, I was in total shock, mainly because just a few days prior to today, she and I had been laughing on the phone together. And the three of us had already purchased tickets for an upcoming trip to Jamaica to celebrate the Thanksgiving holiday! Now the crazy part was that Mama, Stanley, and I knew cancer. We'd all worked at University of Texas MD Anderson Cancer Center, so we knew it all too well! And we knew about pancreatic cancer too. We knew that the prognosis sucked! In that very moment, I knew that Mama would die soon.

So this is where my grief journey began—on a telephone call with my dying mother. It is interesting because prior to November 2012, I always fantasized about the journeys I would take in life. I often thought of my romantic journey through dating and into marriage, my journey through my blossoming career, my journey within my dearest friendships, and my journey through womanhood and motherhood. As naive as it may seem, it never dawned on me that one of my life's journeys would involve death, pain, heartache, and pure lamentation. Furthermore, I never anticipated that my mom—my confidante, my best friend, and my rock—would die so young. *She was only sixty-three years of age.*

> As naive as it may seem, it never dawned on me that one of my life's journeys would involve death, pain, heartache, and pure lamentation.

I had just left choir rehearsal and was driving home to simply relax and enjoy a peaceful Saturday. Being the extreme doer that I was at the time, I recall immediately shifting into fix-it mode, exploring my memory bank of treatment options from my prior employment at a cancer treatment facility. I thought of the endless hours I would spend researching expert physicians across the country, treatments for pancreatic cancer, in-home care for my mom, and employment positions in anticipation of my move from California back to Texas. I decided that I would move in with my mom and work alongside my brother to be there for her daily. I even considered all of the things I needed to do at work, home, and church to prepare for my move.

All of this mental aerobics occurred within seconds of my mom sharing the devastating diagnosis—*stage IV pancreatic cancer*. Yet, my plans for aggressively pursuing my course of action following our conversation ended abruptly when my mom calmly stated that she did not plan to pursue any medical treatment. She said that the doctors could offer her "comfort chemotherapy," but she refused. My mom cried briefly with me on the telephone that day—for the first and only time after receiving her death sentence. She knew what the diagnosis meant.

Ironically, she had worked for more than a decade at a major cancer institution, caring for patients with all types of cancer diagnoses. Nevertheless, despite the fact that medicine and technology had advanced since her employment there, she knew that her days were numbered. My mom had also served for more than two decades as a nursing instructor, preparing students to care for patients in similar situations as her own. However, this meant nothing as she lay in her hospital bed. I could only pray that the nurses and doctors with whom she interacted were as diligent, observant, and compassionate as she was throughout her nursing career.

In addition to my mom's current predicament, my family had also experienced the deaths of several family members and friends to aggressive cancers in the preceding four years. This took quite a toll on my mom's emotional state, largely because the majority of the deaths were unanticipated and fast-paced. When my mom spoke of the individuals who had died, I could always sense a quiet solemnness in her voice. Against this backdrop, my mom expressed a desire to live out the remainder of her life at home with her two children and with other things dearest to her—her six-year-old beagle, Bundy, her favorite movies, and her living space. These had always been the things she cherished the most, particularly after her divorce from my father a few years prior to the diagnosis.

Though difficult to explain, my mom's tempered communication about her final wishes grounded me in that devastating moment, and I knew from that conversation forward what I needed to do. I needed to suspend my longing to fix the situation, to dissect every detail, or to wrestle with my mom to change her position. I simply needed to be in the moment, something that was foreign to me at the time. The fight in me subsided as I embraced my mom's peace—a peace that truly surpassed my human understanding. My mom knew that I was the identified crier in the family, and I believe in my heart that she needed me to simply be present with her without my tears. Lord knows I would *definitely* have plenty of time for that later!

Just as I felt myself crumbling under the pressure to remain strong for my mom on the phone, she informed me that her medical team had entered her hospital room, and she needed to go. She said she loved me, and I said the same. She placed the telephone back on its base, and then silence ensued on my end. It was a type of silence I had not experienced prior to that moment—one where time seemed to stand still. I sat on the side of the road in my parked car, helpless to say anything, helpless to do anything—even helpless to pray at that moment. What immediately followed after my mom and I ended our conversation were vision-blurring tears. The only words I could mutter beyond my tears were "Jesus, Jesus, Jesus."

I sensed cars passing by me, and I wondered if the drivers or passengers had a care in the world. I recall observing some people laughing and smiling, while others seriously peered ahead at the road. Suddenly, I felt angry. How could the world be laughing and carrying on with its daily routine when my mom was dying? Didn't anyone care what was happening to her? To me? To my family? Why couldn't someone notice my pain and pull over to care for me in my heartache? How could my mom be dying at the age of sixty-three? What the hell was God thinking? The barrage of questions that flooded my mind, coupled with the realization that life did not stand still for my mom (or me), opened an even bigger floodgate of tears. I do not recall how long I sat in my car and cried that day. I do know, however, that my eyes stung when I finally opened them, and the sun's rays beating against my face felt like fire.

The next voice that I heard on the other end of my cell phone was my dad's. I have no idea what transpired in our conversation beyond my informing him about my mom's diagnosis and current health status. What I do remember is that he wholeheartedly listened to my words and endured my tears without reservation. Somehow, I made it home safely that day. I opened the front door to my house, walked in, bent down to scoop up my beagle, and lay across my bed with him, allowing my incessant tears to soak the top of his head. A barrage of questions, coupled with confusion and frustration, flooded my mind. *Stage IV pancreatic cancer … with no evidence of symptoms beyond mild upset stomach in the months prior and jaundice only a week ago?* How could my mom, who had already dealt with two divorces, a hysterectomy, Crohn's disease, and a series of mild strokes, now have to face this deadly disease? Why her? Why me? Why now? What was God thinking? What now? I lay there, paralyzed to speak or act for the rest of the day.

###

The next few days of work and other nonessential things were largely a blur. The end of the fall semester was approaching, and typical of that time of the semester, my workload as a professor was steadily increasing. My fall teaching schedule consisted of four courses, each requiring my extracurricular time and attention. Teaching, grading, checking e-mails, answering telephone calls, interacting with students and faculty, advising, reviewing manuscripts, preparing for professional conference presentations—these were my ongoing tasks. And this did not even include my work in private practice, where, ironically, I counseled children and families coping with end-of-life matters.

My sleep-wake cycle deteriorated with each passing day, as the moments leading up to sleep were filled with my pacing the floor, communicating incessant prayers to God (actually, *begging Him* for my mom to live), crying, fighting through general restlessness, and experiencing agitation (about anything and everything). At any given moment, I could have exploded. And those around me knew to walk on eggshells and interact with me in the most sensitive way.

Despite the two-hour time difference, I would phone my mom in the hospital, sometimes awaking her, just to hear her voice. Selfish? Maybe. But I felt comforted that she was still so alive, in spite of her rapid descent into death. Each time we spoke, I could not detect the slightest hint of fear, anger, or sadness in my mom's voice, though I constantly listened for it. My training as a psychologist made it quite difficult for me to ignore my attunement to every word my mom said, as well as the way she said them. I literally clung to each breath, each sigh, each pause, and each change in her tone of voice. I listened as if to receive some sort of confirmation that she would survive her death sentence. I even envisioned a time when she and I would be able to reflect upon her diagnosis and treatment, as well as celebrate her survivorship.

> I literally clung to each breath, each sigh, each pause, and each change in her tone of voice. I listened, as if to receive some sort of confirmation that she would survive her death sentence.

Because of my vision, I spent every waking moment after work researching everything I possibly could about pancreatic cancer. I learned that by the time individuals were diagnosed with stage IV pancreatic cancer, the possibility of cure was slim to none. I learned that only 6 percent of individuals diagnosed with this type of cancer actually survived. I learned that the length of time from diagnosis to death varied from one month to less than six months. Basically, when I did finally fall asleep in the wee hours of each night, it was just about time to wake up and prepare for the next day. I was averaging about two hours of sleep per night, followed by ten-hour workdays! I can confidently say that is *only* by God's grace that I actually made it to work on time and tended to all of my responsibilities without error.

My sole focus in each moment, however, was flying home to actually be with my mom. In the immediate days following her diagnosis, my brother visited her daily in the hospital and shared updates with me about her health via telephone. He comforted me and encouraged me to finish up things at work, typically saying, "Mama will be fine." I relied upon him as a brother, as well as a nurse, his chosen profession. As I attuned to my mom's voice, I, too, listened to everything spoken and unspoken by my brother. And I spoke with my mom as many times a day as possible, still searching for some tone in her voice that would let me know that she was, in fact, fine. So I counted down the days until I would be able to go home.

Each day that I spoke with my brother, I could tell that he was scared of what was yet to come. I was too, though we both chose to focus on considering her recovery and healing in our conversations, despite our mom's decision to forego medical treatment. *I knew, however, that she would die in December 2012.* In the midst of one of my many restless nights, after I had prayed for clarity about the situation, the Lord presented me with a specific date in a dream, December 7, 2012, the day I believed would be the day of my mom's death. God so clearly revealed the date in the dream that I knew not to challenge it, question it, or plead with Him for a different date. It was the first time in my walk with God that I *heard* His voice so clearly in my spirit! And it was not loud or invasive like I had previously thought it would be. Rather, it was calm, even, and precise. My reaction to this revelation, quite disparate from the way I thought I would react to such news, was steadiness. I pressed forward each day, armed with my mom's death date.

I never shared this revelation with anyone, especially my brother. God had shared it directly with me, and I felt that if He wanted my brother to know the date, He would share it with him too. Perhaps this was selfish at the time, but I did not want to alarm my brother any more than my mom's health status already had. And because it was the first time that God had spoken to me in such an unequivocal way, I did not want to overstate things or add more confusion to an already stressful situation (*even though I knew it was God's voice*). So in our daily conversations, my brother and I only talked about our mom's eating and drinking habits, noteworthy bathroom experiences (yes, urination and bowel movements), interactions with the medical team, and her overall physical status. My mom and I also spoke as often and as long as possible via telephone every day. She continued to manifest a calm presence, and even armed with the date, I felt a strange sense of peace as well. It was the same peace that my mom exhibited each time I spoke with her, a manifestation of Scripture. "And the peace of God, which surpasses all understanding, will guard your hearts and your minds in Christ Jesus" (Philippians 4:7 ESV).

Throughout week one of my grief journey, God was already planting a seed of faith in my heart through my mom. Little did I know just how desperately I would cling to this seed in the days, weeks, and months to come. For the second time in my adult life, I realized that I *desperately* needed God like never before. Truth be told, I had not ever *fully* leaned into God for much throughout my life. Though I had endured a challenging childhood, I had experienced many mountains growing up, interpersonally, athletically, and academically. Further, my young adulthood had been marked with tremendous blessings in many areas. My favorite response to God in my adult life was, "Thank you, God!" as He opened many doors and allowed me to experience things that most people my age had not experienced. So while I attended church faithfully and also engaged in many ministry activities and prayed daily, my relationship with God was not *fully* developed. I had mastered the art of including God in my life on a part-time basis, as opposed to upholding Him as a full-time Father and treating Him as such. This was a situation that I could not control, no matter how desperately I wanted to, and it would require me to exercise *total* dependence on the Father, whom I had not developed a complete relationship with! I knew about Him, and I had even experienced moments with Him; however, I did not fully grasp the totality of who He really was in my or my family's life. Without Him, however, I knew I would not survive the incredible race set before me!

> I had mastered the art of including God in my life on a part-time basis, as opposed to upholding Him as a full-time Father, and treating Him as such.

When I learned the day that my mom would be discharged from the hospital, I decided to fly home to surprise her and support my brother in person. I wanted more than to hear my mom's voice on the other end of a telephone line. I longed to touch her, smell her, and finally see her with my own eyes. At that point, I would not have to rely upon voice cues to assess her health. I would be able to look directly into her eyes and simply know without a shadow of a doubt. *I could not wait to fly home!*

###

November 17, 2012

Well, I'm in Phoenix at the moment, at the airport, en route to Houston. I flew out from Ontario early this morning. And OMG, I can't wait to see Mama later today! Well, I can ... but it's a trip I have to take, even though I don't want to! My thoughts are in a complete whirlwind, and I can't seem to stop recounting all of the events that have occurred in such a short period of time!

It's absolutely crazy! On November 3rd, Mama drove herself to the doctor and waited at the emergency room. She had noticed yellowing of her eyes (jaundice), and being a nurse and former nursing instructor, she knew this was a problem. She was admitted to the hospital that day. Four days later, on November 7th, Stanley's birthday, she underwent an ECRP (a procedure to check her intestinal tract). On November 9th, my brother contacted me to discuss the possibility of cancer. And on November 10th, Mama called me to share the official diagnosis of stage IV metastatic pancreatic cancer. On November 13th, I was informed that Mama would be discharged home on hospice today, November 17th. What the hell? I feel like I'm in a twilight zone can't escape!

So I'm flying home to be with my first love, my mom. It's the hardest flight I've ever had to take. I want to be with her, but a part of me knows that being with her means that I'll have to face the hardest thing I've ever dealt with in this life.

It's crazy that a part of me is happy for her. I mean, as believers of Jesus Christ, we pray and ask to be in the Lord's presence ... the holy of holies. We ask to feel His presence, hear His voice, and see His face. And Mama will have a chance to do all of these things. She will *live* with the Lord! Since her divorce in 2004 (actually before that), Mama had begun to struggle emotionally. She felt alone at times, as well as heartbroken. She began to view life in a more cynical way. Her brother had died shortly before that, and Granny's mental status began to deteriorate prior to her being transferred to a nursing home facility. Then Mama suffered a series of strokes in 2006. This really changed her! She bounced back a little and returned to work part-time in 2007, which was good for her. Overall, her physical health was fine, but there was a sadness about her. I began to listen more to Mama in our talks and realized the heartache she'd felt about her divorce, her relationship with Granny, and her health issues. She decided to stop working in 2010 and downsize her lifestyle. That's when she decided to move out of her house into a comfortable apartment in the same area. She was physically okay but still heartbroken. This year, in March, she suffered a second set of strokes, from which she physically recovered again. Emotionally, she continued to struggle though, more worried about her financial status in the coming years, Granny's ongoing deterioration as a result of Alzheimer's disease, and adjustments to her recent stroke. Looking back now, I can see that her heart was completely overwhelmed. So while I am so incredibly sad about things right now, I believe that the Lord knew this too. Maybe He knows how overwhelmed she is and wants to spare her from any more pain? Who knows?

This life is filled with so many hurdles! There is comfort in having a relationship with the Lord. He knows that Mama has endured so much in this life—two divorces, a hysterectomy, Crohn's disease, ten mini strokes, and now cancer. And this doesn't even include all of the internal stress she probably faced while wrestling with life's issues. And of course, listening to my drama, LOL! Well, I believe God said, "That's enough, my child!" This is the end, and I'm okay with that. Mama will finally be able to *rest!* No more worry, no more stress, no more pain. How could I be upset about that? The tears I have shed are about her not physically being here. Who the hell am I going to cry to now, complain about dating, share my dreams, fantasize about the future with? I don't know. But I'm happy that Mama will finally get what she's craved for so many years. And that's peace! God is still good as far as I'm concerned. I'm so, so sad, but at least I know what she'll be in the care of the one who created her in the first place.

Well, I need to call Daddy quickly before I board the plane. Up, up, and away. To where, I have no idea. God, keep me ... please.

Looking back on this journal entry, I cannot help but see the strength of the Lord present in my weakness. How was I able to feel so calm about my mom's death? James 1:12 continued to resonate in my heart around this time. *James of all books in the*

Bible! This was one Scripture that prior to this moment in my life, I would read and think, "You've got to be kidding! Count it all joy when you face *trials*? Receive a crown after enduring a *test*? *Really?*" My mind and heart could not fathom how anyone could endure heartache and pain, yet be able to *consider* joy of any kind! *And the thought of God passing out exams as an indicator of life mastery was just absurd!* Nevertheless, I read and reread this Scripture, trying to make sense of it in some way.

"Blessed is the man who perseveres under trial, because when he has stood the test, he will receive the crown of life that God has promised to those who love Him" (James 1:12 NIV).

"Anyone who meets a testing challenge head-on and manages to stick it out is mighty fortunate. For such persons loyally in love with God, the reward is life and more life" (James 1:12 MSG).

As I meditated on James 1:12, I got it for the first time ... the proverbial *it* that believers long for. In my case, *it* was a personal understanding of how Scripture related to my present circumstances. For the first time, words printed in Scripture became manifest and tangible in my life. And the focus, interestingly for me, was not on "the test" or "receiving a crown." I really did not care about the credit I would receive for passing a stupid test! My focus was on facing this enormous and life-altering challenge *head-on*, actually *standing* the test and *meeting* the challenge! As I read the Scripture, I knew that God was telling me that I would have no choice but to face my mom's impending death with my shoulders squared back and my eyes straight forward—focused squarely on the reality of His presence in the midst of her dying. I would have to actually show up to the meeting—a meeting where I would need to be wholly present, acknowledging the fact that my mom's days in this life were shrinking with each passing momen. This was what my mom had done across so many tough situations in her life. She called it "putting on big girl panties!" She *always showed up!* From my volleyball tournaments to pep squad to band practice to college gatherings to cry fests and drama, my mom was always there for me ... without hesitation or complaint. I had no choice but to stand tall, walk straight into the fire, and see what awaited me there.

Sounds crazy, I know! The visual that continued to come to my mind at the time was a roller coaster. If you have ever been on a roller coaster (especially if you have sat in the front cart), you know the feeling of being able to see what's ahead—the inevitable fall. Yet, you know that you cannot do anything about it. You are securely fastened into the cart, and no amount of protest will change your fate. You anxiously sit there, taking in each "click ... click ... click" you hear on the track, and anticipate the long and inescapable descent. Your heart races, and your breathing becomes shallower as you cycle between inhaling and exhaling within each terrifying moment. And as you recover from each drop, your heart races. You try to collect yourself and start all over again in preparation for *the next*. Despite your attempts to pump the brakes and stop the fall, you descend rapidly into what seems like a never-ending abyss, screaming and yelling at the top of your lungs, clenching the bar in front of you! You close your eyes and hold your breath, waiting for the wave of panic to subside so that you can feel normal again. Well, I was literally seated in the front row of a ride that I had never been on before, a ride that I never thought I would not be on at thirty-seven years of age! *Click ...* her symptoms. *Click ...* jaundice. ... *Click ...* hospital admission. *Click ...* stage IV pancreatic cancer. *Click ...* no treatment. *Click ...* hospice. And the worst click of all ... my mom's death.

> I was literally seated in the front row of a ride that I had never been on before, a ride that I never thought I would not be on at thirty-seven years of age!

I had not really considered my life without my mom prior to this moment in time. I always knew that she would be front row and center at my wedding, celebrating an answered prayer along with me. I always knew she would be an active (*okay, nosey*) participant in her grandchildren's lives! I always knew that she would continue to applaud the pivotal moments throughout my growing career. She had always been my biggest fan, my cheerleader. *Now, in a warp-speed fall, I was literally clinging on for dear life, watching my mom's life rapidly come to an end. It just made no sense.* No sense at all! As I reflected upon the timing of everything, I could not believe how much had occurred within two short weeks! Hospital visit to hospital admission to a stage IV cancer diagnosis to home hospice in ten days! God gave my brother and me *no choice* but to face the music! With the fast pace of everything, we simply had to keep going. Home hospice was our new reality, and that was that! *All we could do was stand!*

###

November 25, 2012

Today has been completely exhausting! It's 10:25 p.m., and I am just now sitting down to journal. My friend and I went to church this morning and then enjoyed lunch prior to coming back to Mama's house to rest. I was almost falling asleep at the restaurant! I'm sitting here now, feeling sleepy and overwhelmed.

After church, Mama and I talked about Thanksgiving a few days ago. She really enjoyed the time we spent with her siblings and other close family, our Greenwood side. We had such a great time, and Stanley and I captured some nice photos of Mama with the family. Mama reminded me again today that this was her last Thanksgiving, and she was okay with that. At this point, she has talked about her impending death so much since beginning home hospice a week ago! She wants to be a part of every decision Stanley and I make. She will be cremated. She will have a small memorial service, and she will not have anything pink as part of her service. Her wishes! It cracks me up a bit that Mama, even in her final days, is steering her own ship in so many ways. She is definitely a woman who knows what she wants and does not want! I really love that about her!

Tomorrow, Mama will meet again with hospice personnel. I believe the clinical social worker will come over this time. From what I understand, the social worker will continue to help Mama sort through her final arrangements and discuss plans for long-term hospice. Well, as long term as "long term" will be. I really don't think Mama has much longer to live, based upon my revelation from God a few weeks ago. It freaks me out to think that she will not be here in a few short weeks! Sometimes, I wish the Lord had not shared December 7th with me. But I cannot escape the sense of knowing what I feel deep down. I know that the clock is rapidly ticking away.

Anyway, that's enough talk about death, cremation, memorial services, funerals, etc. *Enough already!* Night!

After two weeks of discussing death, my mind was overloaded. Even though I knew the realities of my mom's approaching death, discussing it every day with her proved challenging. For the first time in my newfound journey, the weight of death's load felt incredibly heavy. I literally felt fatigued and emotionally drained. *How could my mom discuss cremation and memorial service planning from sunup to sundown?* She was so incredibly comfortable discussing all of the nuances, ranging from what she wanted her urn to look like to people she preferred to see at her memorial service to the amount she wanted my brother and I to spend on everything. On one hand, this really helped us get things in order. My mom was quite the organized bird, so it was fairly easy for us to pick up her *script* and run with it. Looking back at the pace of it all, there is no way that we would have been able to coordinate everything needed without my mom's detailed guidance.

So there were moments when the death talks were comforting and necessary. At other times, however, they felt burdensome and awkward … like in the middle of watching movies together! One morning around this time, my mom and I were watching a Tyler Perry movie, one of my mom's favorites. Following one of the scenes where a female lead discovers her love for one of the male leads, my mom responded in wonderment about how short life is and the need to experience love before you die. Of course, this then enabled her to enter into discussion about the death zone again.

I understood, yet resented death at the same time. If love were so necessary in this short life, why would God allow the person who I loved more than anyone to leave me? Who would love me like she did? Who would get me like she did? These were questions to which I knew I would obtain no answer. So I simply held my breath through our death talks, enduring the discomfort and growing frustration for my mom's sake. This was her process, and I respected that. When the doorbell rang and I welcomed the social worker into my mom's home, I felt a sense of relief.

One of the things my mom feared in life, including the days approaching her death, was being a burden to those around her (even though my brother and I assured her that this was not the case). Ironing out the details related to her dying process, I believe, gave her a sense of control during a time when I am sure she felt so helpless and out of control. She also needed to know that she had done everything possible to make things simple for my brother and me, not unlike her approach to parenting over the years. It was during this time that I began to observe my mom as a sacrificial lamb on some level. *She had, in fact, laid down her life in so many ways so that my brother and I could thrive in our own lives.*

When I was in fourth grade, my mom and dad decided that it would be best for me to attend a special magnet program focused on math and science. Despite the fact that the school was forty-five miles away from our home, I remember my mom waking up prior to sunrise and driving me all the way to school and then going to work herself. She sacrificed sleep (and probably other things) so that I could be in a rich learning environment. As a young adult, she often denied herself sleep in order to comfort me in the wee hours of the night, all the while experiencing restlessness from her own emotional and physical health threats. In my mind, her death process was no different. This made me love and appreciate her all the more! Now how her sacrifice would specifically impact our lives, beyond the suffering part of it, was yet to be determined.

On a separate note, my mom began to share interesting windows into death with me, which I enjoyed. On one occasion, it was as if my mom could see others who had previously died in her bedroom. She would point them out to me and ask if I could see them. I would respond that I could not, but I would inquire about who they were. My mom would begin to describe them—what they were wearing, what period in time they were from. *That was neat!* Her face revealed a peace and comfort in her ability to capture a glimpse into the spiritual realm. Spiritually, it confirmed my impression of heaven, a welcoming and inviting place filled with those who had died over the years. I wonder now if that was God's way of reassuring me about where my mom would go after she died.

> Death is the only thing that we will *all* experience in this life.

By the end of the week, I was certain of one thing. Death is the only thing that we will all experience in this life. And I felt comforted by 1 Thessalonians 4:16–18, which says,

> For the Lord himself will come down from heaven, with a loud command, with the voice of the archangel and with the trumpet call of God, and the dead in Christ will rise first. After that, we who are still alive and are left will be caught up together with them in the clouds to meet the Lord in the air. And so we will be with the Lord forever. Therefore, encourage each other with these words.

So maybe my mom saw those "in the clouds" with God. I know that whatever she saw, she felt comforted and calmed, and she said that *they* were welcoming. And so she would be with the Lord forever. At times I craved to see what she saw in those moments, if only to be more connected to the journey that my mom was apparently experiencing.

###

November 30, 2012

Well, despite my thinking about it, I didn't have a chance to write in my journal. I would have never guessed that caring for a loved one would be so physically and emotionally draining. But I don't say this as a complaint! It's simply a fact. Anyway, I flew back to LA today, picked up Hunter, and hit the sack. Today I went to work, which was tough! It definitely didn't take long to get out of the swing of things. But, praise God. Today I accomplished all of my goals. Now I'm relaxing and about to get into my new daily devotional.

As an avid journal writer, I craved the comfort of my journal, as well as its unadulterated acceptance of my most private thoughts. My journal had always been a safe haven, an escape to express myself over the years. In the days following my mom's transition to home hospice, I served as my mom's primary caregiver during the day while my brother worked. A nursing aide visited daily to tend to my mom's personal bathing needs, which my mom enjoyed. She eagerly awaited the hour devoted to taking a hot bath, while at the same time chatting with her friendly aide. I appreciated the compassionate and tender way that my mom's aide cared for her each morning. I also appreciated the hour as a space for me to engage in my own self-care, usually the gym. I lost quite a bit of weight around this time, related in large part to my using high-energy workouts to release the mounting emotional and physical tension that I had observed since my mom's diagnosis.

For the remaining hours that I was alone with my mom each day, I was on high alert. With each personal request, I quickly obliged my mom's desires. I anxiously sat on the edge of her bed, attempting to master the art of anticipation for food, water, TV, anything. On occasion, I successfully predicted her cravings for vanilla ice cream or Campbell's soup, and before she even needed to use any energy to speak, her bowl was there right beside her on the nightstand. In the moments when she slept, I, too, tried to rest, though unsuccessfully. Thoughts raced through my mind, including what might happen if she were to awake and see me sleeping. *How selfish that would be!*

I considered leaving her side to vacuum, dust, or unload the dishwasher, only to remember that most parts of her home remained untouched since her return. I could call someone to talk, though this would affect my ability to focus solely on my mom. I did not want to miss a thing, even if I simply sat and listened to the sound of her breathing while asleep. A slight movement on her part represented hope, potential, and a chance to live in my mind. This is what I told myself, though I knew in my heart that these thoughts were not accurate. So I sat and waited until the next opportunity to hear her voice and experience the life she had remaining. *God, I want to know more of You. I want to know Your heartbeat, Your ways, and Your thought process. I know that the more I know of You, the more I will know about me. Reveal more of who You are to me tonight. Amen!*

Prior to my returning to Texas to care for my mom, an acquaintance at church told me that during this time with my mom, I would come to know God like never before. In the moment when I heard this, I immediately resented her. I resented the fact that she thought she had any sort of glimpse into *my* reality, and I resented her for assuming that I did not already know God. I had always despised others for applying their own life circumstances to mine, as if I would automatically experience my situation like them. Yet, in this very moment, I realized that she planted a seed that she knew would grow throughout this season of my life. *Deep within, I knew that God was stretching me in new directions.* I found myself longing to know Him in a deeper and more intimate way. If I could only understand His ways and His thoughts, I could understand my current reality. I realized that something about my present experience would help me understand who I was. On some level, however, I knew that I would never fully understand His ways and His thoughts. They were higher than mine, and I would have to continue to sit with the uncertainty of it all.

> Deep within, I knew that God was stretching me in new directions. I found myself longing to know Him in a deeper and more intimate way.

###

December 2, 2012

Why in the world did I come back to California? Was I crazy or what? My mom's dying, and I'm 1,500 miles away! I must be a terrible person, for sure! All I can do is muscle through each day and try not to bite anyone's head off. I'm irritable. I'm not sleeping. I'm tired. *Everything* is getting under my skin! Lord, please help me make it through the next few days. In five days, I'll be back home with my mom. I pray that You continue to keep her and bless her, God. This semester is progressing like molasses, and I need to be with my mom. Forgive me for thinking I needed to do anything else, God. Help me make it through the next few days please. I just want to get through the day, avoid anything that will get on my nerves, and fly home. Simple. Thank You, Lord.

Why did I return to California following Thanksgiving after all? That question haunted me for quite some time. Knowing me, it was my attempt to conquer all things in my world. Ha! Just the thought of this makes me laugh and cringe now! Given my predisposition for controlling things, this was probably my attempt to live under the guise of control in the midst of feeling so out of control. Heading back to California in order to tidy things up for the semester perhaps gave me a sense of purpose and a space to make a difference. This was not something I had felt while in Houston. Of course, I had provided care for my mom, which did make a difference. And, yes, this fulfilled a purpose for her and me. But I (perhaps selfishly) needed to experience something more tangible. I needed to know that my actions would lead to an identifiable product of some sort, and I knew this would be the case at work. After spending two weeks in a nebulous emotional and spiritual bubble, I needed to know that my works yielded something. Now I realize that my need to achieve something was rooted in my performance-based lifestyle. In order to feel accomplished, I needed to *do something*.

I had always struggled with James 2:17 (NLT), which says, "So you see, faith by itself isn't enough. Unless it produces good deeds, it is dead and useless." Having faith in the midst of my mom's dying simply was not enough for me. Without producing something tangible, *I felt dead and useless*. Yes, this is a distortion of Scripture, I know! But this is where my headspace was, no doubt.

When asked, "How are you, Mekel?" I would automatically respond, "Just fine." Clearly, however, I was in control of nothing at this point along this newfound journey. I found myself questioning every decision, concerned that I would make a terrible mistake of some kind. My own self-doubts, coupled with growing irritability and sleepless nights, were unbearable. I found myself avoiding others at work for fear that if someone said the wrong thing, I would overreact. Actually, I avoided socializing with most people, afraid that they might look at me with pity, which I despised. I did not want to hear anyone else's stories about caring for dying loved ones or the generic comments filled with sorrow about my plight.

I knew that beneath my calm and collected outward presentation, a storm was brewing under the surface. I had seen the aftermath of similar storms twice before in my life—one at the age of sixteen and one while in college. Both had resulted in collateral damage, both emotionally and physically, so I knew how critical it was to save face at all costs. My energy needed to be directed at caring for my mom, not my own personal uproars. So I experienced each day back in California with frustration, irritability, and edginess in every aspect of my life.

I did not want to hear about how challenging work was when I knew that life was so much bigger than work. I did not want to listen to students complain about their struggles in graduate school when I was experiencing *real* struggles of my own. I did not even have the patience to meet with my own patients during this time. Since my mom's diagnosis, I had transferred my private practice patients to a colleague, recognizing that I could not bear the weight of my own journey and embrace theirs at the same time. In retrospect, I am thankful for this God-inspired insight. I can only imagine the emotional damage I could have caused others in the midst of my own emotional turmoil. *This* was hardcore evidence of God's grace, as well as His strength being made perfect in the midst of my growing weakness (2 Corinthians 12:9). *I could not even help myself!*

My faith waxed and waned, and the Scriptures that I had studied over the years were nowhere to be found. At this point in time, I was simply begging God for all things—sleep, peace, health, my mom's well-being, and strength to make it through each moment. I was taught that begging God was sinful since God already knew what you needed. I thought that previously learned Scriptures would come flooding out of my spirit to create a more peaceful state. I thought that my faith was strong enough to withstand the pressures that I faced on every side. *Yet, relief was not within my grasp.* I often awoke to tear-stained pillows each morning, residue from the prior night's emotional upheaval and residue from each morning's open floodgates.

> I thought that my faith was strong enough to withstand the pressures that I faced on every side.

Looking back, I can see that God was teaching me, however. First, I believe that He allowed my spirit (my will and my control) to be crushed in order for me to move beyond my own strength and into His. I also believe that I needed to see myself (for the first time ever) in a state of emotional and spiritual chaos. This thirty-seven-year-old, accomplished, professional go-getter and giver to many came face-to-face with herself. It was humbling. It was painful. It was ugly. Emotional disarray, confusion, uncertainty, and spiritual mayhem—this, too, was a part of me, I discovered. I despised this, and at the same time, I embraced it as my new reality. *Frankly, I had no choice!*

December 7, 2012

The day that I drove between eighty and 105 miles per hour to make it from Los Angeles to Houston. Yesterday, I got a phone call from Stanley saying that Mama may not survive the day. I made it! I raced down I-10 East to the tollway and then to Veterans Memorial (which was a mess) to 1960 to T. C. Jester. Today, I made it! I was greeted by Carlos and Stanley, as well as Aunt Kim and Aunt Donna, and then I raced into Mama's bedroom to see her lying there peacefully. She knew I was there. She said my name. All day, she'd been asking when I would be there. I made it! I prayed over her with Stanley and Carlos, and then we just sat. I cried a little, but Mama was strong. She spoke some, though her voice was a whisper. I was only able to make out a few short phrases and words. She rested for hours in the same position.

When everybody left, Stanley and I snuggled into bed with Mama. It was peaceful. She kept saying, "I want to go home," and, "I wanna feel safe," so Stanley and I encouraged her to go home. We reminded her that home was safe, where God was, where there's no more pain or stress. We all thanked God that there was such a place called home. And then Mama fell asleep.

December 7th, the day that the Lord had shared with me in a revelation a few weeks earlier. The day prior, December 6th, I woke up and headed to work. It was my last day on campus prior to the Christmas holiday. So my plan was to finish things up at work, fly home, and spend the remainder of December with Mama. Since things appeared to be pretty calm in the days leading up to December 7th, in some ways, I dismissed my prior revelation from God. I'd booked a flight from Los Angeles to Houston on December 7th in the late afternoon. I was very anxious to get home and see my mom.

However, around 4:00 p.m. on December 6th, I received a desperate telephone call from Stanley about Mama's deteriorating health. I could tell by the sound of his voice that I needed to get home *stat!* And, even though I already had a flight booked for the next day (December 7th), my adrenaline kicked in! My attempts to contact my airline only resulted in more anxiety and frustration, when I realized that nearly all of the flights from Los Angeles had extremely long layovers in San Francisco or Phoenix. Out of *all* the times I'd flown to Houston, for some reason, I could not secure a direct flight within a reasonable time frame! *Really, God???* I prayed that a flight would somehow appear and that I'd be with my mom in a few short hours, but nothing. I knew that there was *no way* that I'd be able to think straight or wait around for my flight a day later!

I recall that I was in my office when Stanley called. After we hung up, I frantically raced about my office and scurried to finish up every loose end that I could think of. So many thoughts raced through my mind. *Will she survive until I make it to Houston? Can I change my flight? Did I submit all of my grades? What happens if I don't make it before she dies? Why didn't I just stay in Houston longer?* And the list goes on and on. Angry thoughts toward God also pierced my mind, including the fact that He allowed my mom's health to deteriorate so rapidly when I had just talked with her *that* morning! I raced next door to the department manager's office, fully distraught at that point, and I shared that I needed to leave work right then. I do not remember what he said, but I do remember crying incessantly and literally running from his office to the parking garage to retrieve my car.

Somehow (it was the grace of God, I know), I made it home safely that evening. I threw my car into *park*, raced up the elevator to my loft, retrieved Hunter, my beagle, raced back down to my car, and then began the twenty-four-hour driving trek from Los Angeles to Houston. I did not pack a bag, turn off my AC, turn on any lights, or check my mail. The only thing on my mind was my ailing mom. I recall talking with my dad briefly about my plan to drive to Houston, which he discouraged for good reason. I was in the midst of an emotional upheaval, physically not rested, and spiritually numb. Yet, I had to press on, despite his concerns! *I just knew deep in my belly that I had to start driving right then!*

I can honestly say that my actions that day were completely raw, and I responded out of my flesh. While I frequently called upon the name of Jesus, I did not take any time to calm myself and seek the Father's voice for His will in the midst of all of the chaos. *If anything, the only thought of Jesus that day was how angry I was at Him.* Looking back, I can see that the experience was a great lesson about the *grace* of God. "But God said to me, 'My grace is sufficient for you, for my power is made perfect in weakness.' Therefore, I will boast all the more gladly about my weaknesses, so that Christ's power may rest on me." (2 Corinthians 12:9 NIV)

Weakness was an understatement! Not only was my mind weak from the barrage of worry and stress about the possibility of not seeing my mom before she died, but my body was also physically weak. In the weeks leading up to this moment, I had experienced a fairly regular upset stomach to the point where it was hard to make it work each day. My shoulders constantly ached, and I slept a maximum of two to three hours per night. For all intents and purposes, I was a walking zombie! And to top it all off, my eating habits had deteriorated, with my primary reliance on popcorn and smoothies. I did not eat at all along the drive, for fear that this might provoke additional (and unwanted) stops. My poor dog was relegated to minimal potty breaks as well.

Spiritually, however, I felt pretty strong in the days leading up this moment. My mom's diagnosis, coupled with all that came with it, resulted in my seeking God more regularly than I had previously. I found myself literally feasting on His Word like a fine delicatessen and being met by His loving arms. Further, I had shared the news about my mom with a few close friends in California, and they each encouraged me in different ways. Nevertheless, in the heat of the situation, my spirit was utterly crushed. In my true physical, emotional, and spiritual weakness, God took His rightful place as captain! God's grace was more than sufficient for me, and His power and strength was evidenced in my stamina throughout the cross-country, middle-of-the-night trek.

> In the heat of the situation, my spirit was utterly crushed.

Only stopping for gas and a few quick restroom breaks for my beagle and me, I made it from California to the Lone Star State in nineteen hours! A twenty-four-hour road trip had been stripped down to nineteen hours! The only thing I remember from the trip is praying to the Lord to allow me to make it home before my mom died. In the midst of my frantic and adrenaline-ridden state, all I could think of was the date—December 7th. In my mind, I remember thinking that she would die on this day. And I was determined to make it home, physically be with my mom, and talk with her once more. With tears streaming down my face, blinded to the road in front of me, I made it to Houston!

When I finally reached the city limits, I felt a bit of relief, but I knew that I still had to press! I continued to speed through the city, trying to avoid all traffic, lights, or stops of any kind. *I made it! I made it!* By that point, my brother began to call me more frequently at my mom's request, asking where I was. He would share the telephone with my mom, at which point I would inform her that I was "almost there." I would encourage her to stay awake until I got there, and she would occasionally whisper in response, "Okay."

By the grace of God, I made it! My car screeched to a halt, and I quickly parked and raced up the stairs to my mom's home and into her bedroom. *I have no idea how my beagle even got out of the car!* My sole focus was on my mom! *And I made it!* Words cannot even describe the relief and thankfulness I felt that day! *It was December 7th, and I made it!* I gently hugged my mom, careful not to lean too hard against her frail body. Then I lay across the bed with her, so relieved that she was awake, alert, and aware that I had made it home to be with her. She softly patted my back as I hugged her. She called me by my nickname, "Mickey." I knew that she knew her baby was with her. I cried alongside her, my brother, and my god brother, and I prayed.

God had blessed me so throughout the trip! No food, no sleep, no music. Nothing but simple prayers, eyes focused straight ahead, and a car pressed to its limits! God's grace carried me to Houston, plain and simple! I know that had it not been for His grace, I would not have made it! I could have easily been in a car accident several times, been pulled over by police for flagrant and dangerous speeding, or fallen asleep! Jesus Himself took the wheel for me throughout those nineteen hours! Then He blessed me with my mom's life and voice! *To know that she knew I was with her and to hear her say my name was an unbelievable gift!*

Given the adrenaline rush I had experienced throughout my trek, I did not sleep at all that night. Besides occasional restroom breaks, I stayed with my brother at my mom's bedside. As the day turned into night, I became more and more restless. My recollection of God's revelation about December 7th haunted me as the midnight hour approached. My anxiety stretched to the point that I found myself lying next to my mom to capture her breaths. When she was awake, I would try to solicit a conversation from her. Though my mom was quite weak, she managed to communicate by nodding, looking in my direction, or smiling. At 11:59 p.m., my mom was still alive, much to my relief and surprise. *Perhaps December 7th was a symbol of some sort*, I thought. While confused about the date and what it represented, my attention and gratitude was centered on the fact that my mom was still on this side of heaven. *And for that, I was very grateful!*

December 8, 2012

Well, I didn't sleep last night. My right side is really aching, so sleep was not comfortable at all. This morning has been good. I woke up and straightened up Mama's apartment and then spent some time with Mama. She startled a bit in her sleep, and then she was okay. She wanted water and then ice cream, so I fed her. Then we had a nice chat. She called my name several times and then motioned for me to position here so she could see me. She said, "I did it fast," several times, and I encouraged her to do "it" again. She smiled. ☺ After that, she kept saying, "I'm watching you," and I said the same. I was a little tearful, and Mama picked up on it. She said, "You're crying already?" I told her they were tears of joy. Finally, she said she needed to tell me something, so I listened. All she kept saying was, "Praise God." I sang this song to her and asked if she could see Him. She said, "Yes," but she said she was afraid to close her eyes. She said that she wouldn't see many anymore. I simply reassured here that I would see her again. I don't know if she was being literal or figurative, but either way, it was comforting. I told her that we could both close our eyes together, which she liked. After cheating and being called on it a few times, she closed her eyes and went to sleep. She's snoring now. LOL!

2:48 p.m. Stanley and I are sitting on Mama's bed. He's reading, and I'm writing. She's sleeping now. Around 1:30 p.m., Mama started asking for Stanley.

7:00 p.m. Mama, Stanley, and I are lying down in Mama's room. She had a pretty good morning, but she started getting agitated around 5:00 p.m. She started saying that she was "ready" and "not ready." She expressed feeling a lot of pain and started waving her arms around. We calmed her by talking to her and sharing some of her medication and hot tea. This worked for a while, but then Mama began to stare blankly and groan. After almost an hour of this, Stanley called the hospice nurse, who told Stanley to give Mama some of the Ativan to calm her more. At this point, it seemed as though Mama couldn't close her eyes. This began to tear me up emotionally. I had to excuse myself from the room. Now it's been twenty minutes, and her eyes are closed, praise God. Stanley's reading, I'm writing, and Mama's resting. Overall, it's been a good day. I'm focusing now on Psalm 91.

11:28 p.m. I just finished talking to a friend from church. She's been dealing with some personal issues and needed a friendly ear. It was nice to be able to share some of my challenges, encourage her, and pray with her. Mama's resting more comfortably now, especially since we gave her the Ativan. She's been asleep since a little after 8:00 p.m. Stanley and I are watching *Law and Order: SVU*.

I read and meditated on Psalm 91 (NIV).

> Whoever dwells in the shelter of the Most High will rest in the shadow of the Almighty. I will say of the Lord, "He is my refuge and my fortress, my God, in whom I trust." Surely he will save you from the fowler's snare and from the deadly pestilence. He will cover you with his feathers, and under his wings you will find refuge; his faithfulness will be your shield and rampart. You will not fear the terror of night, nor the arrow that flies by day, nor the pestilence that stalks in the darkness, nor the plague that destroys at midday. A thousand may fall at your side, ten thousand at

your right hand, but it will not come near you. You will only observe with your eyes and see the punishment of the wicked. If you say, "The Lord is my refuge," and you make the Most High your dwelling, no harm will overtake you, no disaster will come near your tent. For he will command his angels concerning you to guard you in all your ways; they will lift you up in their hands, so that you will not strike your foot against a stone. You will tread on the lion and the cobra; you will trample the great lion and the serpent. "Because he loves me," says the Lord, "I will rescue him; I will protect him, for he acknowledges my name. He will call on me, and I will answer him; I will be with him in trouble, I will deliver him and honor him. With long life, I will satisfy him and show him my salvation."

Oh, how I sought the Lord's shelter that evening! In between the moments when I interacted with my brother, you could hear a pin drop in my mom's home. I had actually never experienced that sort of silence before! So I chose to lean into God's Word and dissect this passage of Scripture. I chanted, "God is my refuge and my fortress," in my mind repeatedly. I literally visualized myself standing in God's shadow, much like the shade that a large tree provides in the heat of the day. I imagined God wrapping His wings of protection around me, shielding me from my own fears and anxieties. I would read a few words and then close my eyes to soak everything. Imagining Him in this way felt like I was breathing in fresh air and letting go of my harsh reality.

> I imagined God wrapping His wings of protection around me, shielding me from my own fears and anxieties.

I proclaimed within myself that I would *not* fear the night before me, even though I knew in my heart that it was a critical night for my mom. My brother and I had noticed that my mom's breathing had become a bit shallower and lacked a regular rhythm. And, we could hear that my mom was beginning to experience difficulty swallowing. At some point in the night (between 8:00 p.m. and 11:00 p.m.), my brother raced to a nearby pharmacy to purchase a bulb syringe in order to help her swallow. I prayed while he was gone, mainly that my mom would not die in his absence. I pleaded with the Lord to grant my brother the same grace that He had showered me with throughout my journey across the country. God did, and my brother returned safely. This helped my mom shift into a more comfortable space, after which she rested.

When she fell asleep, my brother and I made a verbal pact to stay awake. My brother, a registered nurse, knew all of the physical signs of death and dying. Calmly and delicately, he described each one of them to me. He also confirmed that our mother was, in fact, actively and rapidly dying. The strength of God erupted in him, allowing him to separate his awareness of the prognostic indicators from the depth of his relationship with our mother. *It is this strength that allowed me to remain calm and embrace the reality that the end was near.* My brother and I prayed together, and then we reaffirmed our promise to one another to stay awake. Strange perhaps, but both he and I wanted to be awake at the time of her death to support her in the transition to the Father. *She had been there when we were born, and we wanted to be there for her when she died.*

PART 2

WHATEVER YOU DO, DON'T HOLD YOUR BREATH!

December 9, 2012

Mama died today between 4:30 a.m. and 5:44 a.m. Wow! Only the Lord knew that she would go home to be with the Lord one and a half days after my arrival. I'm *so* glad I made it! Stanley and I were asleep in the bed with her the entire night. We really intended to stay awake with Mama all night. However, she snuck away during the one hour we fell asleep!

So my brother and I fell asleep after all, despite our desire to stay awake throughout the long night! I suppose our bodies and minds needed rest. And perhaps it was ordained by God that my mom transition to heaven in complete peace without an audience. At 5:44 a.m. (CST), I abruptly awoke and turned to see my mother lying still in the bed. I knew that she was gone! I could tell by the stillness in the room—a stillness I had never experienced in my life. It was as if the air had literally been sucked out of her bedroom! I screamed my brother's name, and he jumped, now alert. We looked at each other, and then the Lord took over. We prayed over my mom, freshened her up, and then lay in the bed with her for a while. After what seemed to be such a short time, the coroner and other hospice personnel came, and my mom was gone. I lay in her bed afterward, caressing her sheets and breathing in the air where she had taken her last breath. The rest of that day was a blur.

What is so interesting about the way my mom "snuck out of dodge," as she would say, is that she seemed to wait to die until both my brother and I were tucked in and quietly sleeping. On some level, even in her deteriorating state, I believe she heard my brother and I express our desire to stay awake at all costs.

And when she sensed that we had fallen asleep, she *fell asleep* as well. *This was my mom's way throughout her life.* She always felt most comfortable in the background, in the shadows, quietly and consistently offering support. My mom was a woman who did not require much praise for her efforts, and she found little pleasure in the spotlight.

The way she died was a reflection of the way she had lived her life. Her dedication to and concern for my brother and me was enormous, and her greatest wish was that we be safe, secure, and able to stand on our own two feet. I suppose that night, somewhere in her conscious awareness, she decided to allow herself to finally rest, knowing that her babes were just fine. In my eyes, it was a fulfillment of God's promise in Genesis 28:15 (NIV), which says, "I am with you and will watch over you wherever you go, and I will bring you back to this land, [home]. I will not leave you until I have done what I have promised you."

> I suppose that night, somewhere in her conscious awareness, she decided to allow herself to finally rest, knowing that her babes were just fine.

My mom wanted to die in her home, and God granted her that. She wanted to die surrounded by her children and most treasured belongings, and God granted her this as well. My mom took her final breath in the sight of God, Her Creator, alone, and she went home to eternally be with Him. *He did not leave her until He did what He had promised her.*

###

December 10, 2012

Home. I was thinking of the perfect title for the poem/expression that I'm going to read at Mama's memorial service. I have to prepare it in the next few days. I was reading one of my friend's Facebook posts, and she shared this word. And *home* was the word Mama used to describe where she was ready to go. Home. Thank you, Jesus.

10:27 a.m. I'm reading my devotional and meditating on the message today—Exodus 16:9–16. It speaks of the Israelites complaining and God reminding them that He is enough. The devotion encourages the need to delight in God's "enoughness." Honestly, I can say that God has provided all of my needs, even in my complaining. During this past month, my thoughts have shifted to focusing on God's provision, especially with regard to Mama. I watched and listened to her express her wishes—to not prolong her death, to not be in pain, to have all of her affairs in order, and to not be a burden. And God heard her cries and answered every one of them perfectly. He was enough for her. She was at peace the day she received the news that she had pancreatic cancer. She was at peace the day she learned that the cancer had metastasized. She was at peace the day she learned she'd be going home on hospice. She was at peace the day she felt 100 percent that she would die at home. She was at peace when she last spoke to Stanley and me. She was at peace. God was enough for her all the way through. And I know He'll be enough for Stanley and me in the days to come. He *is* enough! As I write, I'm crying. I miss her already! She was such a strong person! She held her head high and demonstrated such dignity from day one. She proved that God is enough. He is enough!

Relaxing Into the Pain

11:39 p.m. Stanley and I just got back to Mama's house after a very long day. It started with the agency that had delivered Mama's medical equipment to her house. They arrived to pick up everything around 10:00 a.m. Her bath chair, wheelchair, walker, and toilet seat. Mama never had a chance to even use any of it! Then Stanley and I went to the funeral home to arrange Mama's memorial service after a short breakfast. It was different than I'd imagined it to be, much more peaceful and clear. We ended up deciding on a cremation package, which includes Mama's urn, floral arrangement, cemetery service, written programs, video stream, CD, and faux oil portrait. Stanley and I are satisfied and feel confident that we honored Mama's wishes as much as possible. So her memorial service will be held on Friday, December 14th, at 11:30 a.m. Then we went to see the new James Bond movie, *Skyfall*.

My brother and I somehow shifted into *doing* mode the next day after my mom died—that space where you *must* simply keep going or cease to fully exist. We interacted with the medical equipment company, passively observing a young man pick up each piece of equipment from my mom's bedroom and load it onto his white truck. He tried to engage in small talk throughout his visit, I recall, but I offered no response. I watched him drive away and then went back inside my mom's house, which suddenly felt hollow and empty. How ironic that as swiftly as my mom died, all of the supports provided to her were also removed in haste. *Things were moving so rapidly, and all I could do was observe as a bystander, speechless and helpless.*

> Things were moving so rapidly, and all I could do was observe as a bystander, speechless and helpless.

My brother and I quickly shifted from this business and drove to the funeral home. It was a funeral home that my mom had selected in the weeks preceding her death. After being greeted by two friendly staff, we walked through the menu of memorial service options together and easily arrived at our decision. My mom's desire was to be cremated, so we selected a beautiful pewter urn, followed by a floral arrangement fitted to her liking. She despised pink and lilies, so we made sure to steer clear of these. ☺ We visited the space where her memorial service would be held and then reviewed the procedure for military burial, since my mom was a US Air Force veteran. Because of my mom's meticulous wishes and planning for her own service, my and my brother's decisions were relatively straightforward. All that was left for us to do in the days ahead was notifying friends and family of her death.

I lacked the energy and emotional stamina to call our loved ones, so this enormous task fell on my brother. I listened to him systematically call each of our family members, using the same phrase, "She's gone," over and over again. I longed to better support him in those moments, but I felt numb to respond. So I passively participated in the conversations, trying to take note of anything substantive. *It was a fruitless attempt!* When he finished with the calls, we drove to the movie theater in silence, emotionally unable to discuss the glaring truth in our midst—our mom's death. In retrospect, I believe that the outing helped us disconnect (at least for a moment) from the realities ahead of us and allowed us to simply *be*.

After weeks of doing, my mind, body, and spirit needed to simply be.

###

December 11, 2012

May I be willing, Lord, to bear daily my cross for Thee; Even thy cup of grief to share, Thou has borne all for me." Jennie Evelyn Hussey is the author of the wonderful hymn "Lead Me to Calvary," written near the early 1900s. I stumbled across this song in my mom's CD collection, and the words struck me deeply. Though I had not fully wrapped my mind around recent events, this became my prayer. The word *willing* resonated in my mind, and I realized that how I would grieve my mom's death in the days to come was a choice. I knew that I had to be *willing* to bear this cross, and I had to make a decision whether to view her death as a blessing or a hindrance. The Lord helped me understand that how I perceived the situation would either lead me to or away from Him. It would serve as a crossroad in my relationship with Him. So I researched Jennie Evelyn Hussey's story and learned that she was a Quaker who endured a life of hardship and suffering. I also learned that she was a caregiver for her sister, who was deemed an invalid. On top of that, Jennie herself coped with a debilitating type of arthritis. All the while, she continued to care for her sister, until she herself died in 1958.

I imagine that in addition to caring for her sister, Ms. Hussey coped with the deaths of friends and loved ones closest to her. I imagine that while her sister was alive, she grieved the thought of her sister not living a life free from disability and pain. I also imagine she grieved the loss of experiencing her own personal freedoms, instead electing to serve as a long-term caregiver for her sister and striving to overcome her own physical challenge. Oh, how she must have yearned for a release from enduring daily pain! Yet, God endured it all for her!

Against this backdrop, I listened to the song again, and it gave me more strength to face my own reality. *God planted a seed in my heart that night, a seed of total surrender and acceptance.* Even my cup of grief needed to be placed within the context of Christ's true surrender and forbearance for all of my (and other's) sins. Christ sacrificed everything so that I could live!

And in many ways, I felt as if my mom had sacrificed herself through her death so that my brother and I could live. I think she knew deep in her heart that she needed to hide in the shadows yet again so that my brother and I could more fully experience all that life had to offer. Perhaps she recognized that through my love and dependence on her, I had not altogether realized my potential to love others in the same way. Perhaps she recognized that my relationship with her stood in the way of my wholeheartedly connecting with those who I physically encountered on a daily basis.

Was it too much for God to ask for me bear this experience, a relatively *small* sacrifice on my part? Looking back, I believe that God was preparing me for battle in advance, reminding me very early on that I had the ability, relying on His strength, to get through the most difficult and devastating experience of my life thus far! *I was deeply sad, and I questioned what was yet in store. But for that night, I was comforted.*

> Even my cup of grief needed to be placed within the context of Christ's true surrender and forbearance for all of my (and other's) sins.

###

December 15, 2012

Wow, we made it through this week! It's the day after Mama's memorial service, and I'm okay. Yesterday was wonderful! Family and a few friends attended Mama's service. Then we all spent time eating and fellowshipping at Stanley's house. Family came and went, and we had good laughs! At the service, a few people shared very kind expressions about Mama. Some of my old friends and coworkers also came. That was so kind of them to offer support in that way! God is good all the time!

10:50 p.m. I'm reading Exodus 33:20–21 (MSG), which says, "God continued, 'But you may not see my face. No one can see me and live.' God said, 'Look, here is a place right beside me. Put yourself on this rock.'" I can't *imagine* literally sitting next to God! Wow! Later, the Bible says that God took His position next to Moses like it was His duty to come alongside Moses! That's so powerful!

It was *such* a relief to have made it through my mom's service, both physically and emotionally! Once again, God's grace prevailed and carried my brother and me through the week following my mom's death. I have only a vague recollection of the memorial service beyond the balloon release at the very end. At one point, I also read the poem/expression I had created for her in the days leading up the service, titled, "The Strength of a Mother."

> Your strength as a mother helped you give birth to a baby on March 9, 1975, in the midst of active Air Force duty;
>
> Your strength as a mother allowed you to wake up in the wee hours of the morning to drive your fourth-grade daughter to a magnet school across town;
>
> Your strength as a mother allowed you to work long hours in the day and still cheer at volleyball and basketball games in the evening;
>
> Your strength as a mother helped you sacrifice so that I could have the very best and do the very best in all things;
>
> Your strength as a mother helped you defend you tenth-grade daughter when she got into a fight (well, beat up) a boy at school;
>
> Your strength as a mother allowed you to hide your own tears when your seventeen year-old daughter moved away from home for the first time;
>
> Your strength as a mother helped you survive a hysterectomy and Crohn's disease, in the midst of juggling so many responsibilities;

Your strength as a mother gave me the courage to step out on faith in the career and try new things;

Your strength as a mother helped you not only survive a divorce, but also thrive in the midst of it all;

Your strength as a mother allowed you to say, "Mickey, I support you," even when you didn't agree with me;

Your strength as a mother gave you the ability to survive two sets of strokes, one while driving to work;

Your strength as a mother allowed you to listen to millions of hours of drama and tears related to my "man problems;"

Your strength as a mother said, "Yes, you can," when I was saying, "No, I can't;"

Your strength as a mother allowed you to be concerned about every detail in my life, even when I didn't ask about yours;

Your strength as a mother helped you receive the diagnosis of cancer with your head lifted and eyes focused on the Lord;

Your strength as a mother allowed you to cope with the news of metastasis and hospice without shedding a tear;

Your strength as a mother forced you to be concerned about my issues, even while bedridden;

Your strength as a mother told me to "praise God" in one of our last conversations;

> Your strength as a mother allowed you to rub my stomach with one hand and hold your own with the other;
>
> And, your strength as a mother allowed you to quietly sacrifice yourself while your children slept in the early morning on December 9, 2012.

Even now, the words expressed toward my mom bring tears to the surface. On her death bed, she was concerned for me and my well-being! At a time when she could have understandably been focused on herself, she shifted her focus to me and my needs. She embodied Christ, revealing the sacrificial nature of His character. *It was powerful, to say the least!*

> At a time when she could have understandably been focused on herself, she shifted her focus to me and my needs.

As I reflected on Exodus 33:20–21, I thought of what it would be like to sit right beside God. I considered the reality that we will never see Him face-to-face until we die and that our encounters with Him while living are only a glimpse of who He fully is. I could note my own *tangible* experiences with God up to this point. My mom, through her death, however, was granted the ability to see God's face! What a privilege and honor that is! I can only imagine what that moment will look and feel like! I felt overwhelming joy for my mom, knowing that she would not be subjected any further to the things of this world—stress, poverty, sickness, etc.

It was on this night that my perception and understanding of healing dramatically shifted. It dawned on me that believers spend an enormous amount of time praying to "be close to Jesus," "experience His presence," "be where [He is]," and "draw close to [Him]." In church, we cry and exclaim how glorious it will be to fully rest in God's midst. As a longtime choir member and worship singer, I had sung countless numbers of songs alluding to this closeness to God over the years. Well, in death we experience this! The Bible says "To be absent from the body is to be present with the Lord" (drawn from 2 Corinthians 5:8), and death affords this!

All too often, in the face of experiencing the death of loved ones, believers say that their prayers were not answered. *Yet, 2 Corinthians 5:8 speaks to the contrary, in my humble opinion!* I had prayed for my mom's physical healing, yet she died. I guess I certainly could have viewed her death as God's failure, but instead, I saw it as her "ultimate healing," just not on this side of heaven. Death is the only place you can go where you will experience complete peace. Looking back, I can see that God was preparing my heart and spirit in so many ways! This revelation spoke volumes and shaped my burgeoning grief journey in such positive ways. I knew there would be emotional storms on the horizon, but fortunately, I was not angry with God about my mom dying. After all, she was right beside God, a place where she would be free from life's worry, frustration, and pain. *To God be the glory forever!*

###

December 17, 2012

9:30 a.m. I'm lying in Mama's bed with Bundy, just thinking. I'm thankful this morning for a beautiful day, sunshine, and peace and quiet. It's hard to believe that it's been eight days since Mama died. Strange. I feel fine. I talk about her a lot and am constantly reminded of her, but I'm okay. The morning that she died was tough, as well as her memorial service. But all things considered, I've felt fine. At this point, I can't tell if it's shock or pure grace from God. I know Mama's gone. I know that she's finally resting and separated from all of this life's stressors. I know that! Perhaps that key piece of knowledge is what has kept me going on. Throughout the week my stomach was very upset almost like my fibroids were acting up. Yesterday I was in so much discomfort that I could barely stand! And this was after drinking hot tea, rubbing my stomach, and taking three Bayer pills! It's stress! It felt like someone had a vice grip on my uterus and was squeezing all throughout the day! Ouch! But today I woke up feeling good. No upset stomach or anything. *God is good!*

Ahhhh, there is nothing like a strong dose of the *physical* side effects of grief! Given my doing mode up to this point, I think my body reacted by sounding the alarm in the days following my mom's death. Previously silent and managed uterine fibroids reared their ugly head, leading me to feel quite nauseous and experience several embarrassing public "blood baths." My dad and I had gone to church the day before, and my attention to the message was overwhelmed by stomach cramps to the point of groaning. When I was finally able to stand up, I realized that the bleeding was obvious, not only to me, but everyone around me! My dad gently guided me through the pew to the exit, and I remember wailing in pain on the drive to his house. This had been my norm since my mom's death, yet, I carried on like I needed to.

My body was finally communicating, in such noticeable ways, that I was stressed! I had always loathed the generic saying, "I'm stressed out," assigning it to those who did not have what it took to get the job done. *Yet, here I was ... 100 percent stressed out to the point that everything I had tried so desperately to hide in the days leading up to and following my mom's death—my fears, worries, anger, hurts, disappointment, and confusion—was manifesting on the outside!* I was good at hiding, learning the tricks of the trade in my childhood. Hiding in the shadows is where I had always felt safe and secure. Even as an adult, I embraced the comfort of hiding in my own thoughts, without concern that anyone would peer into or disrupt them in any way. *This was my comfort zone!*

My physical unrest forced me to step out of my safe and known space, however, into unfamiliar territory—territory where I shared my weaknesses and fears with others. I could no longer hide that my body was in turmoil. *This awareness alone caused me great physical distress.*

> ... here I was ... 100 percent stressed out to the point that everything I had tried so desperately to hide in the days leading up to and following my mom's death—my fears, worries, anger, hurts, disappointment, and confusion— was manifesting on the outside!

I was determined to tackle my inner world by remaining in the shadows. It had worked for thirty-seven years thus far, so I could not fathom why it would fail me at this point. After eight days of physical distress, I woke up feeling good. And this was all the evidence I needed to stay the course and remain hidden, *if only for a little while longer.*

December 20, 2012

Wow, the morning after I should have been arrested. Seriously! Oh, what a night! Last night, after hanging out with friends, I was pulled over by a deputy sheriff for speeding. Truth be told, I wasn't speeding at all. Anyway, after being pulled over, the sheriff started finding things to ding me on—my California license, my registration, etc. Crazy! Then "Mikaela" showed up!

Psalm 55:22 says, "Cast your cares on the Lord, and He will sustain you; He will never let the righteous be shaken."

And boy, was I on the verge of being totally shaken! Wow! I hadn't seen that side of myself since 1995, literally! I know it was God who protected me! There's a dark part of me, an angry part that rears its ugly head (obviously, every seventeen years, LOL). I can't even explain where it came from, but it manifested in cursing and screaming last night. And now I feel horrible, physically and spiritually. I have a massive headache, and my shoulders are tight. Spiritually, I am disgusted with myself! I can't believe that part of me showed up in such a foul way! Be angry, yet sin not. *Epic fail!* I talked to my God brother today, and he reminded me that the eruption of my sinful nature just serves as a reminder of how much I need Jesus and how we all carry demons within us that, because of God's grace, are not seen on a daily basis. That was helpful! I guess this episode served as a humbling reminder that I absolutely, positively *need* God! And the rage-filled part of me is still me, as much as I hate that. But I hadn't thought about the fact that we all carry in us a sinful nature that would constantly be unleashed if it were not for God.

Father, I thank You for Your amazing, never-ending, and all-consuming grace! Your grace covers my imperfections, anger, fear, and frustrations. And without it, I would be a complete hot mess! Thank you for reminding me that I need You desperately all of the time! I love You for loving me unconditionally!

Oh, what an occasion this was! It certainly was not one of my finer moments in life, and it *definitely* did not align with any Christian values I had ever been taught! Let me acknowledge that I have deep regret for the events that took place on the evening of December 19, 2012. I have since taken action to rectify the matter, as well as apologize for my emotional and behavioral misconduct.

Now, the unfolding. I had just enjoyed a nice evening with a few friends at a restaurant a few miles from my mom's house. After leaving the restaurant a little after midnight, I headed west on a very familiar street. Though I did not have a far distance to travel, I decided to relax and set the cruise control in my car. I was shocked to notice a few moments later that police lights were flashing in my rearview mirror. Of course, I pulled over to the side of the road and awaited the officer's presence on the driver's side of my car. Was I a bit perturbed at the absurdity of the stop? Absolutely! And yes, I can admit that the attitude I demonstrated toward the officer as he approached my car was subpar. See, I am a principle-oriented person (sometimes, to a fault), and on this particular evening, I was determined to prove the point that I had *not* been speeding!

The officer (whom I later found out was actually a deputy sheriff) asked for my driver's license and insurance, which I readily shared.

He reviewed the documents and then walked to the back of my car. Upon his return to my window, he asked why I had Texas license plates and a California driver's license. I explained my relatively (well, relative in my mind) recent move from Texas to California, assuming this would cease his inquiry. It did not. The deputy sheriff then asked me to explain why I had traveled from California to Texas. At this point I could feel my temperature rising as well as tears welling up in my eyes. I shared that my mom had recently died and that I had remained in Texas to help settle her affairs, expecting that the sheriff would express some sort of empathy for my situation. Instead he remarked that my *excuse* could be better, and then I snapped. *I snapped!*

Though I cannot recall the exact words used throughout our exchange, I do know that it included many expletives and sarcastic comments on my end. I also know that I was screaming at the top of my lungs, all the while crying like a baby. I remember unbuckling my seat belt and exiting my car. I threw open the rear door of my car and thrust a copy of my mom's memorial service program at the sheriff, to which he responded by ripping the program in half. As dramatic as it may seem, it was as if he ripped a piece of me with his actions, and I completely lost all control of myself.

How could anything else happen to make my current situation feel even worse? Didn't the sheriff know that losing the program was like suffering the loss of my mother all over again? The last thing I recall is crumpling the lofty ticket I received in front of the sheriff, offering him a few more expletives, and throwing the ticket into the road—all of that from God's beloved child, in front of God Himself, as well as any stranger who dared to peer into the madness! I am confident that bystanders looked on with their mouths wide open!

In response to my actions, the sheriff asked me to get back in my car and leave the scene immediately. Beyond a stern tone of voice, he did not react in an aggressive or inappropriate way. The *only* reason I was not arrested that night (or even harmed by the sheriff for that matter) was God's grace and protection! There is *no* doubt in my mind that God was with me, even in my rage, and He orchestrated the situation in such a way that the deputy sheriff extended grace toward me, in spite of my behavior! Literally, if it had not been for the Lord on my side, I do not know what would have happened that night!

To add injury to insult, I had forgotten that I was talking to one of my friends using my car's Bluetooth system. And embarrassingly, he had remained on the line and heard my entire manic episode! My friend gently tried to calm me down with his words, though I resisted his efforts and continued in my rage throughout the entire drive to my mom's house. He stayed on the phone with me until I made it safely inside and then offered to come over. I declined the offer, too shaken and humiliated to interact with anyone. In a matter of moments, I transitioned from rage to utter sorrow, suddenly unable to soothe myself or manage my emotional roller coaster. I remember walking into my mom's bathroom, looking in the mirror, and sobbing uncontrollably. *Who was this person staring back at me? What was her name? Whose mouth had uttered all of those foul things?*

I have no idea how long my sob fest lasted. I woke up the next morning, wearing the same clothes from the night before, completely fatigued and defeated. I recall feeling as if I had been in a physical altercation with someone. My joints and muscles ached, and my head was throbbing in pain. *For all intents and purposes, I had been in a fight ... with the deputy sheriff, with myself, and with God!* I fought the idea that the one person who knew my innermost parts was gone. I fought the possibility of living life without my best friend and confidante—my mother. Once again, everything on the inside seemed to be bubbling under the surface, waiting to boil over. I was a walking time bomb, and I had absolutely no control over myself.

> I was a walking time bomb, and I had absolutely no control over myself.

I wondered how God would unravel this mess and settle me enough to make it through my remaining days in Texas. *With all that needed to be done prior to my leaving, I was doubtful that anything would go well.*

December 27, 2012

Today sucked, pretty much from top to bottom! I woke up early and met my God brother and a couple of kids from his and Mama's church at her house. Today was the day for us to donate Mama's furniture to a family at the church. Well, actually, we were supposed to do it yesterday, but that's a different story. Anyway, I got there and helped coordinate everything. Then my God brother informed me that the family I thought he'd chosen was different and that they lived in Port Arthur, Texas, which was about two hours from Houston. Needless to say, I was irritated, mainly because nothing has run smoothly since Mama's service and because I'm worn out from taking care of Mama's business affairs.

Relaxing Into the Pain

8:30 p.m. Oh, crap! Stanley and I just had a big blow-up fight, all because I was upset that he "told me" to walk home from the U-Haul place back to Mama's house in the cold rain. I came back to Stanley's house and proceeded to take a shower and relax. While I was dressing, he knocked on the door to ask what my problem was, at which time I asked him to leave me alone. He didn't. He continued to press to the point, and I ended up screaming at and slamming my hand in anger at him.

10:31 p.m. I just read James 1:19 and Proverbs 14:29. All I can say is "I need a do-over, *for real!*"

The day started off on a dreary note, both literally and figuratively. My body and mind felt cloudy, and it was an overcast day outside. With gray clouds and moisture in the air, the last thing I wanted to do was deal with nonsense of any kind. At this point, my body had made a bit of a rebound from the prior week's events, yet mentally and emotionally, I was irritable, aloof, and over-reactive to even the slightest annoyances. In my interactions with my God brother, I was snappy and more bossy than usual.

The last thing I wanted to do was spend the day shedding myself of my mom's belongings, even though I knew it was the right thing to do. She had delicately cared for all of her belongings, ranging from her clothing to her nightstand to her collection of clocks. Each item had its special place in her home, and boy, would she let you know if it was not in the right place. I used to love to borrow my mom's earrings, in large part because they were made of real gold. She always had a knack for buying the perfect hoop earrings, and I loved the way they looked on my ears. Anyway, just weeks before she died, I borrowed a pair and returned them to her jewelry bowl. However, I did not place them precisely where they had been when I borrowed them, and my mom let me know about it. She picked them up, gently wiped them with a jewelry cloth, and placed them back in their rightful place.

Watching the kids lift her furniture in a way that seemed so hasty and careless annoyed me. I stood there, micromanaging their every move, frequently asking them to be careful, so as not to scratch or dent any of my mother's things. Nevertheless, with one sudden attempt to maneuver my mom's favorite armoire through the front door of her home, they lost their grip on it, causing it to scrape against the door frame. I screamed at the teenagers and then began to cry inconsolably. I am certain that they were disarmed, but no one said anything. Perhaps my God brother had prepared them for the event, or perhaps they simply knew that to speak would breed additional wrath and make me even more upset.

From that point forward, I, too, participated in the lifting, carrying, and maneuvering of my mom's furniture as a way to ensure that nothing else was damaged. Inside, I knew that one scratch did not really matter in the grand scheme of life. I knew that my reactions were completely irrational. Yet, I needed to do something. The scrapes on the armoire and door frame peeled away the scab that was attempting to heal from my mom's diagnosis, her final days, and her death. It peeled away the anger, hurt, and confusion that loomed beneath the surface of my outwardly calm demeanor. *In one quick moment, the emotional wound felt raw all over again, and I despised that.*

A few hours later, I sat alone in an empty house, left with only remnants of my mom's life. Her beloved grandfather clock. Her favorite dishes. Her beautiful jewelry. Her prized rooster fixtures.

Her well-used purse. Pictures. Her CD and DVD collections. My baby clothes and shoes. Her burgundy lipstick. Her perfume. I sat alone with what seemed like only a shell of my mom. *In a matter of a few hours, it was as if she had never lived, and I was emotionally and physically overwhelmed by the thought of that.* Yet, I had work to do. I knew that in a matter of weeks, her home would need to be emptied in preparation for the next life to live in the space. I cleaned, threw away unnecessary and meaningless items, and I boxed things that either my brother or I would keep for ourselves. With each passing moment, anger, confusion, and sadness grew, but that did not stop me. I was still in hiding mode, praying that these inner feelings would soon subside. *I had no real appreciation of the impact of my emotional upheaval on others or myself.*

As I finished cleaning and organizing everything, I headed out to return the moving van my brother and I had rented the day before. After returning it, I called my brother to discuss what time he would be available to pick me up from the van location. Unfortunately, he shared that he would not be able to pick me up as planned, not at the original time we had discussed. This slight change in plans thrust me into an emotional uproar, resulting in my hanging up the telephone in my brother's face and making the decision to walk to his house (approximately seven miles away) in the pouring rain. I could not fathom why he was not helping with the day's affairs the way we had agreed he would. Each rain droplet masked the tears in my eyes and washed away any feeling of sadness that I had buried within. The rain did nothing to drown out my escalating feelings of anger and frustration, however. Truth be told, I can be a bit of a control freak on a normal day. So I know that in the midst of all that occurred on this day, my "control freak" tendencies were heightened. By the time I made it to my brother's house, my emotions were extremely raw, and I knew that it would not take much to tip my emotional scale.

In order to calm myself down, I took a hot shower and barricaded myself in the guest bedroom, praying that my brother would simply avoid me when he returned home. He did not. Upon his arrival, he knocked on my bedroom door and asked if everything was okay. I ignored his inquiry at first and then responded by asking him to leave me alone. See, I knew the darkness that was brewing inside of me. My brother continued to press me and then opened the door without invitation. *From that point forward, I lost control of myself ... yet again.* My mouth became my only way of escape at first, and the words that flowed from it were condescending and biting. Then the rest of my body decided to join the battle, and I responded by banging my hands on the dresser in a full-blown rage. Cognitively, I knew that what I was doing was wrong. *Yet I could not stop!* I was literally out of my mind, viscerally responding to what I perceived as a threat to my emotional safe haven.

My brother stared on, completely immobilized by my hurtful words and actions. I do not remember all that he said, but I do know that he forgave me in the midst of my rage. I could see it in his eyes. Something (I believe, God) allowed him to view me through a spiritual lens, and he responded graciously. My brother recognized that despite what was coming out of my mouth in pure anger, I actually appreciated all of his efforts and knew he was doing all he could do to help take care of my mom's business affairs. Once again, God's grace poured through him, and the conversation that occurred did not affect our relationship in a negative way in the short- or long-term. Thinking back on this moment brings tears to my eyes as I consider God's love made manifest through my brother.

After apologizing to him profusely, all I knew to do was turn to the Word of God. I felt overwhelmed by guilt and sorrow for my actions. This was my second rage episode in a little more than a week, and I knew I needed help. I found two Scriptures—James 1:19 and Proverbs 14:29.

"My dear brothers and sisters, take note of this: Everyone should be quick to listen, slow to speak and slow to become angry" (James 1:19 NIV). "People with understanding control their anger; a hot temper shows great foolishness" (Proverbs 14:29 NLT).

Frankly, reading the Scripture in James 1:19 riddled me with more guilt and shame than I already felt. I knew I should be quick to listen and slow to speak or become angry! *Come on, God! This read like Behavior Management 101!* On the other hand, reading Proverbs 14:29 proved helpful to me in the moment. Here, I focused on the phrase "People with understanding." If people with understanding control their anger, I logically concluded that those without understanding did not. So I asked God what I did not understand. I even looked up the word *understanding* and found this definition: "The process of comprehending or the knowledge of a specific thing or practice" (http://www.yourdictionary.com/understanding). Then I took a step back to more fully comprehend the Scripture. "People with [knowledge of a specific thing or practice] control their anger." It dawned on me that what I needed to become knowledgeable about in order to control my angry outbursts was the "specific thing" that triggered them. *God helped me identify the primary emotion surrounding my mom's death—sadness.* Not only was I sad that my mom was no longer with me, but I was also sad that she would miss every present and future event in my life. I was sad that she would no longer be my cheerleader and sounding board for life's complex issues. I was sad that she would not be able to experience the fruits of her prayers for my brother and me. Deep sadness—that was the specific thing.

It was in this moment that I acknowledged my tendency to simply *do* without sorting out my emotions along the way. For nearly two months, I had operated on autopilot in order to get through each bump along the roller coaster—my mom's diagnosis, her decision to withhold treatment for the cancer, hospice, and her eventual death. I realized that if I did not address my underlying sadness, another anger outburst was inevitable! Thankfully, the Lord had afforded incredible grace thus far. Yet, I knew that I needed to further understand myself in order to reduce the likelihood of more explosive outbursts. I determined in my heart that when I returned to California, I would pursue individual therapy and/or group grief counseling. *As a matter of fact, I made a promise to God that day that I would do my part to help myself achieve a sense of peace.* I was operating in the shadow of God's protection, as well as in an environment with ample support in Texas. I knew that in California, however, I did not have these protections to the same degree. So I needed to put support in place for myself.

> For nearly two months, I had operated on autopilot in order to get through each bump along the roller coaster—my mom's diagnosis, her decision to withhold treatment for the cancer, hospice, and her eventual death.

By the grace of God, all things had worked together for my good, in spite of me. Second Corinthians 12:9 (NIV) reigned true in my life yet again. "'[His] grace is sufficient for [me], for [His] power is made perfect in weakness.' Therefore, I will boast all the more gladly about my weaknesses, so that Christ's power may rest on me." Christ's power, indeed, rested on me! Yet, I sensed in my spirit that He was asking me for more. He was asking me to *activate* the power He had provided me, and the only way to do this was to ask for help, something I had avoided throughout my adult life. The time had come. *Ready or not, I knew that something had to change!*

###

December 28, 2012

Well, I'm happy to report that I didn't curse, fight, or clown anybody today. LOL! The day was great, actually! I spent most of the day with friends. We laughed and reminisced about the past. I love them so! From coming to Mama's service to calling to checking in to hanging out, they've shown their love for me. And I needed that today! Even in my frailties, they embraced me, cried with me, and listened. Just thinking about it brings tears to my eyes. Night!

Oh, the power of support from friends! Little did I know that I needed it so much this day! My brother and I had just celebrated our first Christmas without my mom, a day that, while joyful and uplifting, felt hollow and empty all the same. My poor emotions had traveled 180 degrees and back in such a short amount of time, yet the time spent with friends helped them stabilize for a moment in time. This was probably the first time my friends saw all of me, despite our two-decade-long friendships. See, I was not the vulnerable type. Rather, I had always preferred to be the friend who offered support, as opposed to the friend who needed or received support. I was the upbeat encourager who served as a cheerleader for others during their storms in life. I was the friend who always had the right thing to say, and I offered the shoulder to cry on. *I can imagine that my friends were just as shocked as I was as I talked with them and exposed the most vulnerable and raw parts of me!*

Just the day before, God had impressed in me the need to be transparent and ask for help. Stepping into a situation where my openness was validated and encouraged by those closest to me was so powerful and transformative. *I had never done this before!* In my world, transparency equaled weakness, and I was determined to exhibit strength throughout my grief journey. I never wanted to be *that* person, the one who cried and bemoaned the death of a loved one for days, weeks, and months on end. I recognize this as judgment now, but at the time, this was my biggest fear. Nevertheless, I successfully confronted it that day and was met with compassion, grace, and love.

Though my friends may not have realized it, their actions revealed the heart of God, as well as His love for me that day. Through their kind words, listening ears, and gentle hugs, God was saying, "Mekel, I see you, and I am here with you in the midst of your sadness. I will never leave you or forsake you. I hear your cries, and I am here to comfort you." In addition, what I learned in my interactions with my friends is that vulnerability opens you up to receive the pure and unhindered love of God. *That is something I do not think I had fully appreciated up to that point in my thirty-seven years of living!*

I sensed that this was the beginning of a deeper relationship with God. On December 8, 2012, He planted the seed of vulnerability in my heart and watered it with the love demonstrated by my friends. Now, He was calling me out of the boat, my emotional comfort zone, into a new space of *true and deep intimacy* with Him as well as others. Up to this point, my mom was the only person I had fully allowed "to see into me" (*into-me-see*). *Really, even God had not been afforded wholehearted access to my innermost parts.* I had lived my life in a very controlled fashion, cautious about who could gain admittance into my safe and contained existence. *The most interesting and sad part about this is that I do not know if I really knew me at all.*

God had covered me with His feathers, and I had found refuge under His wings. His faithfulness had shielded me from so many things outside of me and within me (paraphrase of Psalm 91). Yet, He was inviting me to step out from under His protection in order to experience something I had never experienced before—*the breadth and depth of connection! True intimacy.* I tried to anticipate what that might look like in the days to come; however, God disallowed my thoughts in this direction.

> He was calling me out of the boat, my emotional comfort zone, into a new space of true and deep intimacy with Him, as well as others.

I would be forced to confront myself like never before.

###

December 31, 2012

1:12 a.m. One of my best friends, Stanley, and I are sitting here at Stanley's house, laughing. We're listening to online comedian excerpts. Crazy! But I wouldn't have it any other way. I feel loved! I need to be in bed though. Mama's military service at the cemetery is tomorrow (well, today) at 10:00 a.m.

8:10 a.m. I've been up since 6:49 a.m., preparing to get ready for Mama's cemetery service. Stanley and I have to be at the funeral home no later than 9:30 a.m. It'll be a small gathering of family and friends, probably about ten people or so. Anyway, after praying this morning and reviewing a Scripture discussed at church yesterday (Philippians 3), I stumbled upon a passage that I'm going to share this morning (that I had no idea I'd be sharing when I went to bed a few hours ago), specifically Philippians 3:21 through Philippians 4:1.

"[Some] have minds on earthly things. But, our citizenship is in heaven. And, we eagerly await a Savior from there, the Lord Jesus Christ, who, by the power that enables Him to bring everything under His control, will transform our lowly bodies so that they will be like His glorious body" (Philippians 3:21). "Therefore, my brothers, you whom I love and long for, my joy and crown, that is how you should stand firm in the Lord, dear friends!" (Philippians 4:1).

Who is the world would have thought that I would be ending 2012 at a military ceremony in memory of my mom? Well, the military dictates the day and time for such occasions, so December 31st it was! No fireworks. No fancy shindig. No hair and makeup. It would be me, my brother, a small group of friends and family, and a memorial.

I recall that one of the things I dreaded the most that day was being forced to sit through the gun salute and the playing of "Taps" at the cemetery. Every time I watched it on TV, I cried! Anyway, my brother and I arrived at the cemetery, along with a small group of family and friends, and headed to the site for the military honors. Words of prayer opened the ceremony, followed by brief expressions from military personnel. Despite my desire to share the Scripture prepared in the morning, my heart (and throat) said otherwise. I was so choked up by the ceremony that I literally could not speak. My brother received the military flag and shell casings, and I sat looked on in utter silence.

It was the last day of the year, a day typically filled with anticipation of what is yet to come and resolutions of the past. I had no idea what was yet to come in my life, and I did not have anything to resolve. The one thing that I had prayed for resolution about, my mom's healing in this life, was answered differently than I had wanted. I dreaded the thought of needing to return to California in the coming days. I had grown accustomed to the safety and predictability in Houston, as well as the emotional support from so many friends and family. But I knew that just as God had catapulted the sequence of events surrounding my mom's death thus far, He was thrusting me forward into unknown territory, *in terms of my relationship with Him.*

> But I knew that just as God had catapulted the sequence of events surrounding my mom's death thus far, He was thrusting me forward into unknown territory, *in terms of my relationship with Him.*

Once again, I was seated in the front seat of the next phase of a roller coaster ride with God. *How far down would He allow me to fall this time?* I wondered. Would He give me a moment to catch my breath before the next sudden drop? While I did not know that answers to these questions, I sensed that God wanted me to breathe Him in and simply exhale. *What was for tomorrow would be addressed tomorrow.*

PART 3

NEW WINESKINS AND OLD WINE!

Mekel S. Harris, Ph.D.

January 8, 2013

A new year! A lot has transpired since I last wrote in my journal! But for now, I'm focusing on my daily devotion—Leviticus 22:1–8.

11:11 p.m. I got home around 10:00 p.m. tonight. I went to work at 5:00 p.m. so I could move all of my belongings to my new office space. It took a while, but I completed the task, thank God. On the way home, I almost forgot that Mama had passed away and nearly picked up my phone to call her. See, we used to always chat on my way to and/or from work. Of course, thinking about this brought me to tears on the way home. And when I got home, I started looking at pictures taken just prior to her passing, which made me tear up all over again! I miss her so much! Just thinking about her voice saying, "Good morning, dear," or, "How's Huntie?" Man, grief is crazy and so unpredictable!

After all of the happenings in the two months prior, I was now back at work. Eight days prior, I had sat at a military memorial service in silence. Somewhere between then and January 8, 2013, my brother and I sorted through all of the major affairs associated with my mom's estate, and I packed my car for the trek from Texas back to California. My car, filled to the brink with many of my mom's belongings, created a tight fit for my beagle throughout the twenty-four-hour drive.

Everything seemed surreal! Despite everything that had transpired, it was as if my mom had never existed. In thirty days, in the blink of an eye, my mom had received a terminal diagnosis, went home on hospice care, and died in her home. Thirty days! How was it possible that her sixty-three years of living had come to such an abrupt end? My brother and I tended to the majority of her business affairs, cleaned and cleared her home, and packed the keepsakes we each wanted away. I had returned to the real world and its drama, no longer in my safe physical and emotional cocoon.

January 8, 2013, was my first day back in my downtown office. I had made the decision that it was best for me to show up after the majority of faculty had left for the day. I did not want to confront the pity in others' faces as I looked at them. I did not want to hear one more "I'm sorry for your loss" comment from anyone. I did not want to feel as if I were in a fishbowl with others peering into my grief experience—uninvited, I might add. So I chose hiding that first day.

> I did not want to confront the pity in others' faces as I looked at them. I did not want to hear one more "I'm sorry for your loss" comment from anyone. I did not want to feel as if I were in a fishbowl, with others peering into my grief experience—uninvited, I might add.

It was cathartic to transition to a new workspace, despite my resenting the timing of it all. I could not understand why everything in this season of my life needed to be so sudden. Wasn't experiencing my mom's diagnosis to death in a mere thirty days enough? On top of that, God had catapulted me back to California with one swift slingshot, after only spending a month with those closest to me! Now I needed to move two years' worth of belongings from one office to another in a few short hours? It made no sense! I could feel anger rising within me, yet again. But

I pressed forward with the all-too-familiar emotional stoicism and inward frustration.

I recall the difficulty I experienced not being able to talk to my mom at this time. Of course, I would have called her to share every detail about my new semester, from the courses I would teach to my impression of the students to creative classroom ideas. My mom had served as a nursing instructor for nearly two decades, so she fully appreciated the excitement and challenge of a new semester. She always offered pearls of wisdom from her years interacting with students, which I listened attentively to and tried to apply in my faculty role. On top of this, she would have been a sounding board to help me cope with the frustration of having to move to a new office space in the middle of an academic year. *Who does that?* So reflexively picking up the telephone to call her made sense. Well, until it did not make sense! This was the first time (of many) that the reality of her death slapped me in the face. I felt thankful that I was alone, able to release the tears that had been building inside of me for so many days.

Driving home in California traffic is enough, but driving home with a tear-stained face was quite a different animal! One sparked memory sent me into an emotional crying fit for the remainder of the night. It had been exactly one month since I had last heard my mom's voice, and I desperately longed to hear it. One of my biggest fears was that I would forget her voice, so it comforted me that I could still recall things she would say to me, as well as the way she would say them, that day. In my mind, losing the ability to remember her voice would signify that my mom never existed. *Though she was physically absent, the memory of her voice could live on forever.*

###

January 21, 2013

It's been a crazy couple of weeks! I made it through my first week full-time at work (January 14th through January 18th), and then I started feeling terribly sick around the sixteenth or so. It started with a mild cold and then culminated into acute laryngitis! I visited my new doctor today, who confirmed the diagnosis. Prescription? *Rest*, period. Not talking, while crappy on some levels, has had some benefits. I haven't spoken now in about thirty hours, and I feel more connected to God's voice.

Did I mention that my body definitely responded to the stress I had experienced over the past two months? Prior to fall 2012, I rarely experienced physical sickness. As a matter of fact, I often joked with friends and colleagues that I had an "immune system of steel," rooted in my work with children in schools, camps, and hospitals. I joked that nothing could affect my body after exposure to hundreds of germ-filled children and community settings. Yet, just a few short days after returning to California, my body began to break down. It was a metaphor for the emotional breakdown I was experiencing on the inside, really.

Of course, the laryngitis diagnosis reinforced the suddenness of everything around me. One day I was talking, and roughly one week after returning home, I could not speak. What an interesting paradox this was! I had *so* much to say about what had transpired since my mom's death! I had said so much in the days following her death. My emotions swirled inside, creating incredible dissonance, and I needed to release. Yet now I suffered from laryngitis.

Even if I had tried, my vocal chords would not have allowed me to speak, perhaps for good reason. Given the sadness and anger stirring inside of me, it was probably for the best that I could not communicate with my words. My mouth had spewed so many expletives, harsh words, and cruelties toward others since my mom died. I had wounded others with my voice. The Bible says, "Careless words stab like a sword, but the words of wise people bring healing" (Proverbs 12:18 GWT). And boy, had I stabbed a few folks in a short amount of time! Yet in my heart, I longed to offer healing and comfort to others, even in the midst of this terrible season.

Ironically, it was my voice that served as a vehicle for healing throughout my life. I had always worked in healing professionals, offering emotional and resource support to children, young adults, and families. In my faculty position, I used my voice to educate and mentor students. In my private practice, I used my voice to journey alongside others throughout their emotional healing. I often cheered for those experiencing tragedy, heartache, and setbacks in their lives. Others relied on my voice, but it was of no use at that time. God had silenced me.

As I considered my silent position, I began to recognize and embrace the intimacy that God was affording me, at least to some degree. That word—*intimacy*—resonated within my spirit, yet again. I began to ask God a host of questions. "What do You want to see in me? Why do You want to see into me so badly? What is it You will gain through this exploration into me?" The more silent I became, the louder He became. I believe He was forcing me into a posture of listening—the kind of listening that involves complete stillness and waiting. With laryngitis comes waiting for others to speak, as you recognize your inability to initiate or respond via voice. God's prescription was also rest—*rest in His presence, rest in His fullness, rest in Him being enough.*

I had never truly listened to or rested in God. Don't get me wrong! I really *thought* I had listened for God's voice up to this point in my life. I had attended church and done all the right things—the things that Christians are supposed to do to have a relationship with God. I read my Bible daily and spent time reading my morning devotionals and praying to Him. After praying, I even sat still for a few moments, waiting to hear from Him. That was resting in His presence, right? Looking back, however, I can see that I halfheartedly listened just long enough for God to co-sign on the things I desired or the outcomes I created. I thanked God for blessing me after decisions were made without consideration of His will or desire in advance. I functioned as the pilot, and God was my eager-to-please copilot throughout life's adventures. And this had worked well for me!

> I can see that I halfheartedly listened just long enough for God to co-sign on the things I desired or the outcomes I created.

This season was different, however! My voice was silenced, and despite my resistance, God sought to regain His rightful position in my life as pilot. My ailing voice could no longer direct my life's flight. It was the Lord's turn to chart my path, which would involve many midcourse corrections. He was offering me new wineskins to overcome the old and shift me into a new spiritual and emotional direction. The first step was creating a space for Him to speak to the innermost parts of me. *I was terribly afraid of what He would find, as well as what I would discover.*

February 1, 2013

Wow, since the last time I wrote in here, I've suffered the flu, acute laryngitis, and a host of down moments. Honestly, the past two weeks have been horrible! I pushed my body to the edge when I should have rested, going to work every day, singing with the church, working at home. I recovered mostly from the flu/laryngitis symptoms only to experience an emotional plummet for the past week or so. I realized that I have no social support here. While I know a lot of people, people don't *know* me. I've discovered (well, re-discovered) that I genuinely have a compassion for people. And I truly desire to relate with people. However, I know that my role in relationships has always been to give and serve in an unconditional way. Yet, I often do not receive the same in return. It left me wondering what God expects of me. I mean, is there something inherently wrong with wanting to connect with people? I've realized that if I don't pursue others, I'm easily forgotten. Since returning to California, no one has reached out to express concern. Well, that's not true. Yesterday, an old friend called me. It's so interesting, frustrating, and sad at the same time! It never dawned on me how limited my social support in California is until now.

I have no real friends here, only acquaintances and work colleagues. Sad! I've never felt so alone on the earth as I do now. I know God is there, though I've been irritated with Him lately. Mama filled so much of my life, and now that she's gone, I really see how much of a hole there is in my social life here. I'm tearing up as I write this! I'd heard from families I've worked with in the past that the grief journey can be isolating. I never thought it could feel so lonely. You have all of this support around you at first. Then people move on, and the love and concern that seemingly existed is gone in a flash!

It's caused me to question my purpose on some level. I know that God's plan for me includes touching others' lives, as I do in my professional work and in my personal life. And I love this. I have a love for God that I love sharing, which I also know is His will for me. Yet, am I allowed to connect with anyone, platonically or romantically? Do I *deserve* the manifestation of unconditional love in my life? Last week, I felt that the answer was definitively *no*. Not that I don't deserve it, but I guess I'll never receive it. Now, I still don't know. I feel lonely and invisible, like my only purpose is to bless others without receiving anything. No friends, no lovers, no husband, no mother. Nothing! *Invisible.* Yep, that's the perfect word. I get up, go to work, talk with other faculty and students. Yet, no one peers into my world. No one offers a thank you. No one genuinely cares. I know this sounds depressing. But it's how I feel, and I can't deny that. I don't want to spend the rest of my life talking to Hunter and myself. Is that selfish? Weren't we put on the earth to forge connections? Why can't I? (Oh, this sounds like Dorothy saying, "Why, then oh why, can't I?")! LOL … so sad! Thankfully, I've had enough emotional and physical strength to get up and make it to work. I haven't worked out in a couple of weeks. I've found joy in simple things like going to sleep at night or successfully making it through a class I'm teaching. So anyway, I guess that's better than nothing. It's Friday night, and I'm at home about to lay down. Hmph!

Isolated, lonely, and invisible—the three things I never felt when my mom was alive. It did not matter what time of the day or night I called to talk to her. She was *always* available. She saw and understood me in a way that others did not. Returning to California exposed a harsh reality that had probably always been present since I had moved there. I lacked a true connection with anyone. When I moved to California in summer 2008, it was for a year-long pre-doctoral internship. Given the short twelve-month window, I was not intentional in the way I made or cultivated relationships with others. In my mind, it was not worth the effort, since I knew I would be returning to Texas in a few short months. Plus, I was focused on each sixty-hour workweek, and subsequently, I did not build in much time for socializing outside of the internship. I did not even unpack all of my belongings or hang pictures on the wall! That it how confident I was that I would move back to Texas! When I was offered a two-year post-doctoral fellowship after the internship year, I *still* believed that I would return to Texas at the end of the upcoming twenty-four-month experience. I made the decision to unpack all of my belongings and hang a few pictures on the wall at that point. Yet, my social support system continued to lag behind. I attempted to date and then quickly realized that my work-life balance was completely out of whack. Sixty- to seventy-hour workweeks, unfortunately, did not create a fruitful space for a romantic relationship as a result.

Three years into my *stay* in California, I was offered a faculty position there. Yes, I viewed my time in the sunny state as a stay, a sort of bondage situation that I could not escape. Toward the end of my post-doctoral fellowship, I had applied to several jobs in Texas, certain that one of them would prevail. Remember, I was the pilot of my life flight at that time, and a good pilot always knows where she is going! As the rejection letters flooded in, I began to resent California, relegating it to my "time in the wilderness." The Israelites spent forty years roaming around in the desert, searching for God's Promised Land, and I, too felt like I was roaming around in a dry and weary land in California. Of course, the length of the Israelites' journey was impacted by their disobedience and stubbornness to God's plan, but I could not see how this related to my situation at the time.

Needless to say, I was excited about the new opportunity in academia and accepted the offer in California. I had worked extremely hard up to this point in my life and experienced the benefits of wonderful mentorship throughout my graduate program. So I felt energized by the thought of sharing my knowledge with budding psychologists, as well as serving as a faculty mentor. A part of me also embraced the awareness that I, like my mom, would teach others. In so many ways, my mom had inspired me, and I wanted to be like and honor her.

Throughout this season, I readily connected with my coworkers and enjoyed my time at work, but I still found myself returning to my default state … alone. I also attended a moderately sized church at the time, and I was involved in the music ministry. Nevertheless, I had only been a part of the church for a few months and discovered that I did not have deep-seated roots there either. Further, the dating arena continued to remain dormant.

All the while, my mom and I spoke via telephone every day (sometimes, multiple times a day). When I was not working, spending time with my beagle, or sleeping, I was talking with my mom. To be honest, it *seemed* like I had a great network of friends. Looking back, however, I think my mom just did a wonderful job serving as a mother, friend, confidante, mentor, advocate, "boyfriend," and cheerleader! She filled up so much space that I had no time to truly reflect upon what I lacked in California.

Confronting the reality of my mom's absence, as well as my failure to cultivate relationships where I lived, was devastating! I felt ashamed of my inability to recognize the situation for what it was sooner. *For goodness sake, I was a licensed psychologist at this point!* I had missed all of the obvious signs somehow. My complete love for my mom had blinded me to the truth of my secluded existence. In addition, I was reminded of the suddenness of things around me. After receiving two months of ongoing and consistent emotional support from friends and family, I felt (yet again) that I had been thrust into a new and unsupportive space that lacked anything I truly needed. *I felt isolated, lonely, and invisible.*

The realization forced me into a dangerous tailspin, and I questioned everything about me—my purpose, my worth, my need for love, and my understanding of God's character. I could not see that God wholeheartedly cared for me through my emotional pain and isolation. I could not embrace Psalm 139:1–4 (NLV), which says, "O Lord, You have looked through me and have known me. You know when I sit down and when I get up. You understand my thoughts from far away. You look over my path and my lying down. You know all my ways very well. Even before I speak a word, O Lord, You know it all."

> I could not see that God wholeheartedly cared for me through my emotional pain and isolation.

If God really knew me, how could He have allowed me to be so blind? If He really understood my thoughts, why did I feel so alone? If He were really looking over my path, why didn't He help me more? *I had so many questions for God.* Yet, I lacked the energy to truly pursue the answers on this day. I had used all of my strength to simply make it, and I had nothing left. Grief had stripped any semblance of physical strength I had, and all I could do was *rest* ... on a Friday night of all days!

###

February 3, 2013

It's 8:00 p.m., and I finally experienced a breakthrough of sorts today! However, the day started off very poorly. I only slept about two hours the entire night, and I was plagued with shoulder and neck pain, as well as a headache. My thoughts were racing throughout the night, and tears flooded my face on and off. I'd decided that I wasn't going to church or my LifeGroup, and I lay awake, thinking of excuses to tell people. But when the clock struck 9:00 a.m., I felt compelled to go, mainly because of my church responsibilities. I wasn't feeling it, but I knew I had to fulfill my service as an usher and LifeGroup leader. And I'm so glad I did! I heard a life-changing message today—the story of Moses and God's call on his life!

I do not recall the specifics of the message of that day, but I do know that whoever shared the message focused on Exodus 3. The book of Exodus provides the story of Moses being called to lead the Israelites out of Egypt, following their forty-year journey through the wilderness. Moses, a man who stuttered, questioned God's call because of his feelings of inadequacy. Yet, God summoned Moses anyway. This resonated with me that day, related to my own feelings of inadequacy at this juncture in my life. I was leading a small group of women, as part of my church's small group ministry—women I barely knew at this point. And I was only two months past my mom's death date, still experiencing unpredictable ups and downs in my emotions and behavior. I felt uncertain about my ability to lead anyone, given the fact that I was barely leading myself. I felt like an impostor, afraid that one of the women might see how ill-equipped I really was to serve as a leader. My mouth had spewed venom toward others. I had not lived my life in an open and vulnerable way, and I had a list of other sins buried in my closet. But God forced me out of bed that morning, deferring to the commitment I had made to the church and to the group as a whole. So I obeyed.

Hearing the message at church provided the first sense of relief I had felt since returning to California. On some level, I felt like God was paying attention to me and understood how I felt inside. He grasped my insecurities, yet He challenged me anyway. *It felt like He actually cared. Intimacy.* So despite the fact that I felt emotionally and physically exhausted, I leaned into God's strength, and He honored that. *Rest.* Instead of falling prey to my default stance (hiding), I walked into the light and received a word directly from the Father's heart. I caught a glimpse of His caring nature. Though it was an obligation that propelled me out of my house, my "mustard seed" faith and work yielded something good that day. *Oh, how I needed that!*

> Instead of falling prey to my default stance, hiding, I walked into the light and received a word directly from the Father's heart.

February 3, 2013 was a metaphor for God providing beauty for ashes. I had awakened in physical and emotional pain, yet ended the day in relief. I did not know at the time that God was quickly helping me unearth unhealthy ways of thinking and behaving through His Word. He had planted me in a new church with new people and new experiences. He trusted me with His other children, in spite of my operating as a seeming fraud. Like Moses, God dismissed my weaknesses and summoned me to do what He had called me to do at that time. *Only a loving Father would do that!*

###

February 10, 2013

"God is abundant and is only waiting for you to make yourself ready to receive what you truly need." This was my message from God on Facebook this morning. *Hmmm, interesting. I'm making myself ready by relaxing my need to control everything.* Actually, there are so many situations that are completely out of my control right now. I believe God is using these things to remind me more that I have absolutely no say in the course of my life! I'm making myself ready by learning to relax and trust others. The past few weeks have been good examples. Crying unrelentingly in front of others—no control. Trusting the process of the trip Stanley and I are on, as opposed to micromanaging every part of it—no control. Waking up today and simply being—no plan or control.

6:30 p.m. I just finished grading papers and preparing for work tomorrow. Church was good today. The message focused on seeing ourselves the way God sees us–in His image. The associate pastor talked about the ways that we try to cover up/mask His pure image with makeup, control, money, etc. He offered a live demonstration using mirrors to demonstrate the importance of seeing ourselves face-to-face, naked before God, and loving what He created! One brick at a time, God is helping me lay a new foundation for my life! *Control seems to be a major theme!*

On that note, I made a call and set up an appointment for individual counseling sessions. It's time! I can clearly see that God has exposed areas that need to be addressed. With Mama's passing and my variable emotions, the one thing I know for sure is that I have no control over anything. I can't control my feelings. I can't control who is there for me, and I couldn't control Mama's death. It's been a *rude* awakening on so many levels. But it's forced me to take a step back and simply *be*. I've never done that in thirty-seven years! Right now, I'm feeling okay with simply being.

Can you imagine holding up a mirror to your inner self? What would you see? That morning in church, several images came to my mind as the pastor spoke. I saw the me who was kind, loving, friendly, and generous. I saw the me who was angry, irritable, and emotionally explosive. I saw the outgoing and spontaneous me. I saw the insecure and scared me. I saw prior and current sin. I saw growth. I saw forgiveness, and I saw unforgiveness. I saw the image I projected to the world, and I also saw the raw and pensive part of me, the part that craved hiding in the dark. God had always seen me in this complex way. I had always seen myself in a compartmentalized way up to this point. My mind flashed back to January 21, 2013, only twenty days prior to this date. *Self-discovery had begun.*

I could embrace the parts of me that aligned with my image of godliness, perfection, and wholeness. But the splintered and jagged parts of me were difficult to hold. I envisioned a beautiful palate of bright colors representative of who I thought I was—splashes of red, orange, pink, blue, and purple. Yet that same palate also contained dark and splotchy patches, some of which overpowered the vibrant colors.

> I could embrace the parts of me that aligned with my image of godliness, perfection, and wholeness. But the splintered and jagged parts of me were difficult to hold.

This is who I was! This is who I had always been! I stood before myself in church that day, and for the first time, I saw my nakedness. Though I felt stained and ashamed of the mirror's reflection, something in me knew that God loved me, in spite of me. *Something in me also knew that He loved me so much that He did not want me to stay the same.*

So I picked up the phone and asked for help. I remember that moment as if I were dialing the number right now. I sat in my car, cloaked in its seemingly impenetrable shell. I had already located a counseling center near my home, one who offered faith-based psychological services. I keyed in the ten digits and stared at my phone, as if it would magically dial the number on my behalf. I stood in that doorway for quite some time, as tears streamed down my face. *I hated to ask for help.* I felt humiliated and ashamed. I wanted to hide. I knew what hiding felt like, and I feared what awaited me behind the therapist's doors. But God gave me the strength to press the *send* button. It was a Sunday, so I knew that I would not actually speak with anyone, which gave me relief. I left a message and anxiously awaited a return telephone call from my assigned therapist. *I was ready to see into myself—intimacy.*

###

April 4, 2013

10:00 p.m. Here we go again! It was a simple and straightforward day without a lot of shenanigans at work. Then I had my therapy appointment with Amy, which went very well. I was able to discuss reconciling my image of myself as strong with the decision to take off two days in a row from work. I was able to celebrate the celebration of me, celebrate my setting healthy boundaries for myself. It felt good! I really like Amy and her therapeutic style. She's helping me embrace the here and now, wrestle with reconciling parts of myself, and embrace the new journey that I'm on. So it feels good. Anyway, time for bed.

Ahhhh, how do you spell relief? *Therapy!* Just one day after my initial telephone call to the counseling center, I received a message asking when I would be available to come to the center for an initial intake. The coordinator and I agreed upon a time approximately two weeks later, and my first therapy appointment with Amy occurred about one week prior to my thirty-eighth birthday. By early April, I had met with her about five times. I observed something wonderful in her therapeutic style during my first visit. She demonstrated a special ability to listen with empathy, as opposed to sympathy. I did not feel pitied by her. Rather, I felt as if she were journeying alongside me in my grief and curious, as I was, about where the path would lead. This helped me feel connected to another person and less alone on my journey. Though not a friend, she was *my person*, a living and tangible person for me to feel connected to in California.

All I can say is that the timing of everything, in terms of my beginning therapy, was impeccable! It was as if God had prepared the way for me to enter therapy by first allowing me to confront all the parts of who I was. He then passed the baton to Amy, who helped me begin to reconcile all of those pieces and better understand who I was as I traveled along this new and overwhelming terrain called grief. She invited me to celebrate myself, something I had struggled with, in spite of my bad behaviors in the months following my mom's death. She helped me identify the places where I was functioning on autopilot and guided me toward healthy boundaries, which eased my emotional and physical tension.

What was so interesting to me is that in my work as a psychologist, I had done similar things with so many patients and families over the years. I had journeyed alongside others, helping them cope with impending death, as well as its aftermath. Yet I could not help myself. At this point in time, however, I had suspended all self-judgment and simply celebrated the fact that I was allowing myself to receive support. My perception of strength up to this point did not involve seeking assistance from others. Strength involved taking action, appearing put together, and leading others at the head of the pack. I recognized this as a false and dangerous perception, one that could have potentially deadened me even further, physically, spiritually, and emotionally.

I aligned, yet again, with 2 Corinthians 12:9, and God's strength was made perfect in my weakness. I finally realized that my weakness *was* strength, for through it, the fullness of God could be revealed. Continuing to maintain a composed appearance was the easy part, I realized. Allowing myself to surrender and rest in God's peace was the bigger challenge. *I was healing, and it felt so wonderful!*

> God's strength was made perfect in my weakness.

###

April 9, 2013

So today was pretty good. I woke up a little late and made it to work around 10:30 a.m. Then I had a fairly easy day. I did a lot of makeup work since I was out for a couple of days last week. I got home around 8:00 p.m., and then I went to work out for an hour. I came back and took a shower, and now I'm about to relax and read my Bible before bed. Today I didn't ruminate on frustrating things. I focused on the fact that I've raised $125 for an organization dedicated to pancreatic cancer, which is awesome! I'm on the way to reaching my goal! It feels good to honor Mama in this way, and I haven't cried for a few days in sadness. I consider this a good thing, as I've been able to channel my grief in a constructive way. Anyway, time to get some reading in.

The fruits of my labor in therapy were becoming more and more apparent to me. One of the coping strategies that Amy discussed with me was finding more healthy outlets for my sadness, frustration, and anger. Since my mom's death, the flickers of anger still loomed within, and I continued to operate in turtle mode (that is, hiding) in order to avoid conflict of any kind. It was my way of protecting myself from ... myself. Ironically, I found refuge in my aloneness, largely because I did not have to hide my feelings of sadness in order to make others feel comfortable. I despised being *that* person in the room who dampened everyone's spirits when discussions centered on mothers, births, and joyous occasions with family. I sensed the silence that ensued when I did share that my mom had died. It was deafening and awkward. So I hid.

I showed up to work each day and interacted enough with coworkers and students to appear normal. I attended church as usual, as well as volunteered in the ministries I was involved in. I responded to telephone calls and voice messages just enough for others to not panic about my absence. And of course, I knew just what to say to make others feel relieved for doing their due diligence toward the sick and shut in. This part was easy. I had learned how to save face and play the "put together" role across settings. Yet, I continued to struggle to break through this barrier enough for me to reach out to others beyond my therapist, as well as for them to reach in to offer help.

About a month prior to this time, I stumbled upon the Pancreatic Cancer Action Network on a social media site. It was an organization dedicated to providing support to those diagnosed with pancreatic cancer and their families. As I researched the organization, I learned about opportunities to volunteer, participate in local fundraising events, connect with other individuals via fun runs, and even pursue leadership positions in my local community. So I placed a telephone call to the organization and began to prepare for a fun run event in May 2013. This effort made a *tremendous* impact along my grief journey! I ran more regularly, as I perceived each step as a step in memory of my mom. The exercise served as a source of stress relief and encouraged some sort of connection with the outside world.

As of April 9, 2013, I had raised $125 for the May event, and I was thrilled that my $500 goal might actually become a reality. I finally found a way to honor my mom, as well as help others and myself. With each dollar raised, my mom's life had purpose. She mattered again. Her memory awakened. Others in the organization with whom I connected asked about her. They were not afraid to talk about disease, coping, death, and grief. I remember talking with one young woman around this time whose mother had also died from pancreatic cancer. She and I connected at a community-wide outreach event for pancreatic cancer. As she discussed her grief journey since her mother's death, I related to the sleepless nights and general sadness that she described. I *finally* had a tangible space to talk about my mom without fear of the awkward stares, pauses, and silence. God had provided an outlet for me to relieve the pressure I felt inside, and I felt lighter and freer. I had cried so many tears of sadness since my mom's death. Yet, my sad tears had somehow transformed into tears of understanding and peace.

> I finally had a tangible space to talk about my mom without fear of the awkward stares and silence.

God also reminded me of another emotional outlet for my grief during this time—a children's bereavement camp that I had been involved in since 2010. Over the years, I had served as a group facilitator for children and adolescents, guiding them through the process of sharing their stories of grief, opening their hearts to new ways of coping, and encouraging them to explore a space to create meaning out of their loved ones' deaths. Yet here I was, unable to do any of these things. Again, I was overwhelmed at the thought of sharing my vulnerability in such a public way. Nevertheless, in my mind, I explored how returning to camp might actually provide a way for me to honor my mom and help others facing what I knew all too well.

Looking back, I can see God's attempt to relieve some of my internal pressure. While my emotions were still at a boiling point, I felt less irritable and on edge. *He cared for me, and He was carrying me through the roughest terrain I had ever traveled.*

April 13, 2013

I just had a three-hour conversation on the phone with one of my cousins. She was my mom's first cousin and a great friend to Mama as well. They used to chat on the phone every Saturday. Anyway, she reached out to me on Facebook just to check in. And I decided to give her a call tonight. I'm so very glad I did! She and I talked about so much, ranging from Mama's life and death to her father's life and death to what was happening with her children. I cried as I thought about how awesome Mama was and how much I love her. I miss her voice, and I wish I could talk to her. My cousin said that she occasionally gets visits from her dad in her dreams. So now, I can't wait to go to sleep. I hope to meet with her in my dreams!

Someone reached into my experience, someone who intimately knew my mom. Others had attempted to draw me out of my shell up to this point, no doubt. But I gently refused their advances. They did not *know* my mom. How could they *truly* appreciate my memories of her or understand my reactions in her absence? My emotional walls were virtually impenetrable. But on April 13, 2013, my cousin entered the deep emotional pit where I had comfortably hidden for more than four months. She not only peered in, but she sat down with my sadness. She greeted my heartache with open arms. She invited my anger to not only rear its head, but also rest comfortably in the space.

I was emotionally naked for the first time since my mom's death, and I felt seen and comforted. I applauded my decision to accept help beyond therapy. My cousin had called and left a message, and I had to do my part to activate the healing process. Jesus's command to "pick up [my] mat and walk" rang loudly in my spirit. "The sick man answered Him, 'Sir, I have no man to put me into the pool when the water is stirred up, but while I am coming, another steps down before me.' Jesus said to him, 'Get up, pick up your pallet and walk.' Immediately the man became well, and picked up his pallet and began to walk" (John 5:7–9 NASB).

> I was emotionally naked for the first time since my mom's death, and I felt seen and comforted.

I identified with the sick man's perspective. While I wanted to experience God more fully, I was tired. Grief's vice grip held me tightly, and I lacked the strength to do anymore than I was already doing. I knew that I had taken steps to help myself. At the same time, I knew there was so much more work to be done in me. *I was tired.* But God said it was time to get up and do something different. It was time for me to stop retreating into myself and take steps toward someone other than my therapist. It was time for me to walk into the unknown, uncomfortable space of vulnerability. So I walked through the door that God opened with my cousin that day. Like the sick man, I felt immediately well, which I shared with my cousin. God's love felt palpable. *His love was not a faraway idea or thought. It was tangible!*

###

April 21, 2013

Today's message at church centered on David, prior to his being appointed as king. He lost his family and all of his belongings. Yet in the midst of if all, he focused on the Lord first and strengthened himself. And instead of reacting to his circumstances, he remained centered on God's Word and direction. *This* is the type of Christian I want to be—centered, focused on God, and firmly rooted in the Word (and not my emotions). I'm thankful that the Lord has helped me temper my emotions throughout the past few weeks. I'm not crying as randomly or becoming irritable as often. So I thank God for that. Without Him, I'd be more of a mess.

Lord, tonight as I sleep, I pray that You will quiet my spirit and allow me to draw nearer to You. Allow my mind to be at complete rest, and help my body follow suit. I want to sleep peacefully through the night. Though I continue to wake up around the time Mama died every night, I pray that this night will be different. Instead of waking up and thinking of her, allow me to see her in my dreams. Thank You, Lord, for hearing my humble request. May You bless and keep me, my family and friends, Hunter, and my church family. Good night, Father!

God was drawing me closer to Him more and more each day. By this time, I had experienced the hand of God along my grief journey, and He had reinforced the efforts I had made to pick up my mat and walk. I know that He strategically helped me get to a place of full surrender—when I was completely worn out—because He knew that I would resist things around me otherwise. I was undoubtedly a persistent (some might argue, stubborn) person, and a closed door only served as a signal for me to knock even harder. Yet, my knocking up to this point had only proved to drain my physical, emotional, and spiritual person. As I began to lean further into the Lord, He met me. I felt more emotionally balanced than I had since my mom died. Self-judgment still lingered, but my self-acceptance about how I was coping as a whole was growing with each passing day.

Sleep continued to elude me, however, despite the growing pharmacy in my medicine cabinet and tea collection in my kitchen. You name it, and I had it within reach at bedtime. It seemed like the more I pursued sleep, the more it ran away from me. My mom's death time, sometime between 4:45 a.m. and 5:45 a.m. (CST), served as a marker for my body, a signal that it was time to focus on my grief even more than I had throughout the day. As I approached bedtime, my mind began to magnify thoughts surrounding her death, and my breathing became shallower. Images of my mom lying next to me in her bed lingered, creating a nonstop loop filled with anxiety, avoidance, and pursuit. I desperately wanted to see her in my mind's eye, yet

I battled to avoid recalling this final image of her. Of course, this contributed to many restless nights and an exaggerated sense of the length of each workday. Though I fought to force my body into a restful state (via exercise, music, lighting, medication, relaxation exercises, new bedding, etc.), it rejected me at every turn. Balance was nowhere to be found, despite my efforts to reset.

> Images of my mom lying next to me in her bed lingered, creating a nonstop loop filled with anxiety, avoidance, and pursuit.

It had not dawned on me that one of the reasons for my body's remarkable alert system was that I slept alongside my mom when she died on December 9, 2012. She wanted to be close to her children in her last days, and my brother and I wanted the same. So we cuddled in next to her late on December 8, 2012, and remained in our respective places on my mom's bed until we awoke to her lifeless frame early the next morning. I lay with my back to my mom while sleeping, after which I suddenly awoke, turned around, and soaked in the stillness in her bedroom. I observed her in that moment, taking in every detail of her face, body, and position on the bed. In the days shortly after my mom's death, this image was fleeting, and my memory bank allowed me to focus more on the days leading up to the morning of December 8, 2012. Yet four and a half months after her death, the image of her unresponsive body remained firmly etched in my mind—a still shot frozen in time.

Amy and I wrestled with the image as a source of trauma, one that I was not comfortable considering. She outlined the symptoms associated with a post-traumatic stress response, and I could not deny that my presentation neatly aligned with many of the symptoms she noted. But how could being with my mom as she took her last breath be traumatic? *She was my mom!* How could observing her spiritless person be so impactful? As a psychologist, I knew that Amy's line of inquiry was valid. But as a patient, I questioned her thought process *every* step of the way. Over time, however, our discussions offered a likely explanation for why I woke up at the same time of my mom's death each night and struggled to return to sleep after waking. A host of over-the-counter sleep medications and teas from all around the world could not erase the image carved in my mind's eye. I could not will the image away, or even pray it away for that matter. From this point forward, Amy and I embarked on a path to disentangle my visual memory of a single moment in time from thirty-seven years of beautiful and sacred images of my mom. *Amy certainly had her work cut out for her—that's for sure!*

###

May 1, 2013

3:20 a.m. I've been awake since 2:00 a.m., playing around on Facebook. I woke to the sensation of my stomach growling. Sucks! Anyway, I thought I'd so some journaling instead of just lying there. The crazy thing is that I actually did a progressive muscle relaxation exercise before bed! Guess that didn't work! My body is truly unique, to say the least. This was even after an hour-long workout session, a thirty-minute walk with Hunter, and a hot shower!

Well, I've started to consider this 3:00–4:00 a.m. wake up time as a space to think about Mama and talk with God. The timing coincides with the time she died—around 5:43 a.m. (CST). So for nearly five months now, I've awakened around that time pretty much every day. At first, it felt incredibly frustrating. But the other day, it dawned on me that God may have been answering my prayer to talk with Mama all along by waking me up each day. Pretty cool stuff, if you really think about it!

Using some of the strategies Amy and I had discussed in therapy, I started to reframe my middle of the night wake up calls. Now that I accepted them as a source of trauma, I knew that I needed to disassociate my physical and emotional responses from that final lingering image of my mom on December 9, 2012. *But first, I needed to stop resisting.*

As I awoke and experienced the arousal associated with seeing my mom that morning, I resisted looking at the image in my mind. It was odd, but staring at the image again would only serve to solidify my mom's death. I knew she was gone and did not want another reminder of this. Yet in my heart, I felt inspired to actually look her in the eye and talk with her, as a way of acknowledging and confronting her death head-on. I recalled the Scripture, "Yes, we are fully confident, and we would rather be away from these earthly bodies, for then, we will be at home with the Lord" (2 Corinthians 5:8 NLT). This afforded me great comfort. I could look at her body and at the same time, I could reconcile the fact that the mom I knew and loved was not there. She was with God, and I had nothing to fear or be anxious about. I also remembered my mom's words in the days leading up to her death. *She had said that she wanted to go home. That's* what she meant! God had honored her desires, and she was finally at home with our Father. So I chose to couple the stillness of the night with a host of other memories of my mom.

I reenacted the moment that I awoke to my mom in bed and then forced my mind to consider other moments with her. Funny images, as well as serious moments, came to mind. I began to laugh, talk, and cry with her. I shared the day's happenings with her. I prayed to the Lord and listened for His still, small voice. I inquired about what it must be like for my mom to finally be at home with Him. What did it look like? What was she doing? Who was she talking to? Could she see me? I began to see the beauty in my conversations with her and the Lord, as opposed to focusing on the disturbing nature of one solitary moment in time. My mom was free, and I, too, wanted to be free to remember all of the wonderful moments I had shared with her. *I realized that freedom was, indeed a choice, that I had to make.*

> My mom was free, and I, too, wanted to be free to remember all of the wonderful moments I had shared with her.

###

May 2, 2013

I made it! That's all I've said all day. I made it! I made it through five months without my mom. I made it through an entire semester (sixteen weeks) of grief, all in the midst of ongoing drama at work. I made it through an entire five months of night of sleep that were only three to four hours long, as well as lots of emotional ups and downs. I made it to the end, and I did it quite successfully! I called in sick for only three days, had a few heated tensions with folks, missed a few deadlines, but *I made it!* And I give God all the credit! Without His strength, there's no way I'd be here today at the finish line! Wow, I made it! It literally felt as if I were racing to the finish line this week, gasping for air, but pushing to cross the line. Mama would be proud of me. I can hear her saying, "You go, Dr. Harris!"

After almost five months of traveling along my grief journey, I felt a sense of relief. I continued to feel overwhelmed and emotionally off balance at times, but I also experienced God's stride alongside me. I somehow managed to attend to life's responsibilities, albeit with a few missteps, in the midst of my own life-altering challenges. This was the lifestyle my mom had maintained throughout her life—facing life's issues head-on, in spite of her own difficulties. Only months prior to her death, my mom suffered another series of mild strokes, leaving her physically and emotionally frustrated. She noted challenges with "the little things," like playing her favorite video games (which required her use of refined fine motor skills) or walking her dog, Bundy. Naturally, she experienced moments in her physical recovery when she felt overwhelmed and fatigued. But it did not stop her from doing everything she wanted and needed to do.

> I continued to feel overwhelmed and emotionally off balance at times, but I also experienced God's stride alongside me.

One of her favorite pastimes was playing cards with family and friends. It did not matter what time of the day or night that our family arranged a card-playing tournament. My mom was there! She and her VW Beetle hit the road, and my mom laughed and played until it was time for others to go to work the next morning or for her to return home to take Bundy out for a much-needed walk. I recall so many times when my phone would ring anywhere from 3:00 a.m. to 6:00 a.m., and I would awake to hear my mom's voice saying, "Mickey, I'm home," after one of her outings. She also enjoyed playing bingo with one of her friends, and even after her last set of strokes, no fine motor challenge could prevent her from manipulating multiple bingo cards! It is quite comical to think about now! ☺

May 2013 marked a shift in my grief journey, however. After rejoicing in God's grace, which enabled me to make it thus far, I also began to embrace the reality that my mom would no longer be my cheerleader (at least not audibly). I could still hear her cheering me on in my spirit, but she would not be available to celebrate triumphs alongside me in the flesh. I was not sure what to make of this at the time, so I chose not to focus on it. Instead, I embraced the relief that surrounded me on all sides. *I could finally breathe!*

###

May 26, 2013

So I'm excited! I just woke up and had to document the fact that I saw Mama in a dream! Apparently, she purchased two new cars—an Audi sedan and an SVU of some sort. Anyway, I opened up the garage (to someone's house), and she tried to pull the Audi in. However, she ran into the garage wall upon entry. Then when I told her to back up, she ran into the front of the other car. I spent the rest of the dream rearranging stuff in the garage to help Mama fit her cars in! Other people were helping as well, though

I can't remember who they were. So I didn't interact with Mama or hear her voice. But at least I saw a glimpse of her smiling face! I'm so, so happy!

Oh, what a moment! Almost six months after my mom had died, God finally blessed me with the opportunity to interact with her in a dream! I had prayed that this happen throughout the spring, and my prayers had finally been answered! Fortunately, my brother had already experienced my mom in a dream (or perhaps, several dreams) prior to this point. I was happy for him, yet I longed for my own interaction with her. So as silly and meaningless as the dream seemed, I felt a connection with my mom. She appeared happy, and she was smiling, which provided me with more relief and comfort that she was, indeed, with God.

The next day, I shared my dream with Amy, who celebrated alongside me. The way she discussed the occurrence was interesting, however. Instead of simply accepting my dream at face value, Amy explored what my thoughts were about the *timing* of the dream. *Why* had I dreamed of my mom at this specific time in my grief journey? Of course, I had no idea why. I chalked the experience up to God answering my prayers throughout the spring. While acknowledging God's sovereignty in the situation, as well as His response to my prayers, Amy sensed that there were additional reasons. One of the things she and I discussed were the contexts in which each of us dreams. She explained that while dreaming occurs frequently, the recollection of a dream requires that our bodies achieve their most relaxed state.

Amy recounted all of the sleepless nights I had experienced in prior months, celebrating the milestone that dreaming represented. She affirmed that I had taken steps to help my mind, body, and spirit relax and confront the anxieties that loomed surrounding my mom's death. She applauded me for managing the discomfort of it all, helping me unlock God's healing along my journey and experience a brief connection with my mom. *Then Amy asked a pivotal question that would change the course of my grief journey, and life as a whole, forever. She gently asked, "Mekel, what would it look like for you to relax into the pain of your mother's death?"*

I countered Amy's gentle inquiry with an angry stare and silence. How *dare* she ask if I was willing to relax into pain! What did she think I had been *doing* during the past five months? Did she think that grief was straightforward and painless? She clearly didn't understand me or my situation! After nearly four months, weekly appointments, and hundreds of dollars, Amy knew me no better than anyone else! How *dare* she use this devastating experience to shame me! How *dare* she! I left that therapy session feeling deflated and emotionally spent. *I had no idea what God was doing or where I was going, frustrating my experience all the more.*

> "What would it look like for you to relax into the pain of your mother's death?"

PART 4

So This Is What Rock Bottom Feels Like!

Mekel S. Harris, Ph.D.

June 9, 2013

"Tomorrow's bridge is a dangerous thing; I dare not cross it now. I can see its timbers sway and swing, and its arches reel and bow. O, heart, you must hope always; you must sing and trust and say: 'I'll bear the sorrow that comes tomorrow, but I'll borrow none today.'"

I'm sitting on a plane heading to Phoenix and then Maryland. It's grant review time again. I'm sitting here quietly with so much sadness in my heart. There's no other description that seems fitting at the moment. I feel sad, mainly related to how lonely I feel. Mind you, the past months have been emotional with a handful of events that reminded me of Mama—Mother's Day, a pancreatic cancer run, cancer society commercials, Mama's birthday. So I know that some of the way I feel simply has to do with the reminders that my *constant* is gone. She represented and was so much in my life—a place that I could always fall, a voice that always responded. I can't think of one instance that Mama didn't readily answer or quickly return my telephone call when I called her. Now I have no one—no one who is constant at least. It's like my life is filled with moments in time (snapshots almost) of good connection with others. But the constancy is just not there. I feel like—no, I *know* that I have no one to lean on for constant support.

It's this crazy emotional space where I feel so vulnerable, so needy, and so lonely. As I write this, tears stream down my face. All the while, I'm hoping that no one sees me. Thank God the plane is pretty empty! Add this to the fact that I feel so separated from God! I know He is with me, and I can trace His hand across moments throughout the past six months. It's the *constancy* that I don't feel—the second-by-second experience of God that I desperately need! I recently listened to a broadcast about the book of Job. He lost everything—family, friends, livelihood, security. Not to sound melodramatic, but I feel like Job! I feel like I'm a butterfly flowing in the wind with no aim, no anchor, no security. This is one of the reasons I got my tattoo. Besides loving butterflies, it symbolizes the way I've felt since Mama died—free floating, going with the flow, subject to the changing winds. At the same time, it represents freedom to begin anew.

I'm like a child, crying in angst, with my arms outstretched, waiting for God to pick me up. I'm tired, I'm weary, and I'm lonely. Help me, Father! *You're the only friend I truly have!*

Now at this point in my life, I had traveled around the world on several occasions. And I had never experienced a time when only a handful of passengers were on a plane. As soon as I sat down in my assigned seat, I actually wondered why the flight was occurring, given the low passenger turnout. Yet there I was. I was positioned near a window—seat 16A. I carefully stored my carry-on bag in the overhead bin and settled into my space. I secured my seat belt across my lap and then glanced around. I looked across the aisle to see a row of empty seats. I glanced toward the back of the plane and saw a few passengers settling into their spaces. The typical hustle and bustle of airplane boarding was replaced with the sound of the air vents roaring in the cabin coupled with the occasional overhead announcement by the flight crew. I peered ahead to the first-class cabin, which was generally full. That was it. The pilot's announcement about the flight sequence and plan for takeoff startled my shifting thoughts, and then it happened.

One of the airline crew made eye contact with me and asked if everything was okay. In retrospect, perhaps I appeared a bit taken aback by the scant flight or life in general at that point. *In my heart, I knew I was not fine.* But who actually says that to a flight attendant she has never met, a virtual stranger? *Certainly not me!* I thanked her for her concern and politely declined her offer of support. I could see that she was well intentioned in her attempt to render aid. Nevertheless, I had an overwhelming sense that I was on the verge of crying at the point of her offer. I recall that my eyes began to sting and that tears began to well up. So I did what I knew to do in that moment. I placed my strategic travel hoodie over my head and began to cry. I describe the hoodie that way because throughout my travels, I had used it as a symbol to communicate that I was not interested in interacting with anyone. It was my way of subtlety and kindly saying, "I do not want to be disturbed."

On this particular day, however, my hoodie provided me with a safe haven, a shield, a hiding place to express my pain and sorrow. It afforded me a barrier between my feelings and the world. Truthfully, I did not cry throughout that entire flight. I wailed in pain. The grumbles of sorrow that I had not truly allowed myself to express since my mom's death met me on that airplane and engulfed me in a vice grip from California to Maryland. I could not escape grief's tight grasp, no matter how hard I tried. By the time the plane landed, my hoodie was soaked with tears, my head ached from it all, and I was physically and emotionally spent. *I had officially hit rock bottom!*

> The grumbles of sorrow that I had not truly allowed myself to express since my mom's death met me on that airplane and engulfed me in a vice grip from California to Maryland.

Throughout the flight, I had planned to prepare for a professional meeting scheduled in Maryland, as well as rest prior to the daylong experience. *I managed to fail miserably at this mission.* Instead of preparing for the work-related event, I focused my thoughts on my hotel arrival. I knew that I would not be productive, given the way I felt emotionally and physically. So I anticipated that a hot shower, pain reliever, and a flavorful chamomile tea would at least afford me a good night's sleep before the meeting day. *I could not have been more wrong!*

Upon arriving in my hotel room, I continued to spiral down emotionally, to the point where I was literally curled up in a ball on the side of my bed. I vacillated between this fetal position on the floor, lying prone on the bed, and pacing the room for hours! At times, I continued to cry incessantly with no words. At other times, I literally screamed out to the Lord, pleading with Him to settle my mind and heart. Still, I found no solace or comfort. Close to midnight, I called one of my dearest friends, one to whom I knew I could reveal my true sorrow. And he listened without judgment, encouraged me in prayer, and indicated that I could call back at any point throughout the night to talk. This calmed me down enough to release some of the tension I was carrying in my mind and body.

Yet I still could not sleep! Around 3:30 a.m., I could think of nothing else to do but open my Bible. I lifted it from my purse and thumbed its pages, unsure where to turn or what to read. I prayed that God would somehow will me to turn to the perfect page for comfort. *God did not do that ... exactly!* What He did do was calm my mind down long enough for me to recall a story of a young boy who, like me, was riddled with sorrow and despair. He reminded me of this young boy's call to God, a cry for help. God allowed me to reflect upon the young boy's desperation, which was so much like my own. Through these thoughts, He encouraged me to review the familiar story of David in the book of Psalms—Psalm 56 to be exact.

> You have seen me tossing and turning through the night. You have collected all my tears and preserved them in your bottle! You have recorded every one in your book. The very day I call for help, the tide of battle turns. My enemies flee! This one thing I *know: God is for me!* I am trusting God—oh, praise His promises! I am not afraid of anything mere man can do to me! Yes, praise his promises. I will surely do what I have promised, Lord, and thank you for your help. For you have saved me from death and my feet from slipping, so that I can walk before the Lord in the land of the living. (Psalm 56:8–13 TLB)

I nearly gasped out loud as I read Psalm 56. I was literally tossing and turning throughout *that* night! And I had cried so many tears in the months prior, as well as that day! David exclaimed in his pain that God was for Him, which was hard for me to grasp in the moment. But that did not matter. What mattered was the promise I had made to God in December 2012. David said he would do what he had promised and thank God for His help. *I had promised to do my part to help myself in the midst of my pain.* I did this, or so I thought. I had initiated therapy, as I had promised, and I had worked through so much throughout the spring. But I sensed in my spirit that God was telling me that I had not *fulfilled* my promise to Him. *I had not finished what I had started.*

> I sensed in my spirit that God was telling me that I had not *fulfilled* my promise to Him.

Through it all, Amy's words loomed in my mind—*relax into the pain.* I had not engaged her attempts to schedule an appointment with me for more than a week. *Did she really think I would tolerate having my grief experience mocked in the name of therapy?* On top of this, how unnatural it was to actually relax in the midst of discomfort! Yet, I had made a promise to the Lord. *As I sat on the hotel bed and focused on Psalm 56 that night, I knew in my heart what I needed to do.*

###

June 10, 2013

I cried so much last night that my eyes were literally stinging all the way through the grant meeting. I don't know how I made it through this day! Wow, I just heard a quote on TV that said, "I have all this grief inside and nowhere to put it." That's perfect and precisely describes how I feel. This is the absolute lowest I've ever felt in my life!

Anyway, after today's meeting, I desperately needed to lie down. It took everything in me to make it through—headache, mental anguish, and all. I took an hour-long nap and then ventured out of the hotel to get some fresh air. So, to wrap it up, God saw me through the day. I still feel gloomy, but I made it another day. The rain woke my senses up and helped me feel alive, for the first time in quite a while.

It was so important at this point along my grief journey that I simply make it through each day. It was as if each work-related moment provided me a space to come up for air, despite the fact that it was followed by utter fatigue and exhaustion. I had so much emotion bottled up inside, yet it had no lingering escape. Work, church, and occasional social outings offered relief, though sadness, frustration, and anger loomed just beneath the surface. *My feelings had never sunk so low before in my life!* I thought I understood heartache, sadness, and despair, related to my work over the years with children and families who had experienced devastation, including loss. However, I found that my work with others did *nothing* to prepare me for the emotional abyss I experienced in June 2013.

I found myself engaging in constant self-evaluation, monitoring my own depressive symptoms. As a psychologist, I knew the warning signs for major depression and other psychological disorders. Suicidal thoughts? *No.* Fatigue? *Yes.* Disinterest in pleasurable activities? *Sometimes.* Irritability? *Absolutely.* Changes in eating patterns. *Sometimes.* Sleep disruption? *Yes.* *Self-diagnosis—grieving.* Amy and I had discussed her diagnostic impressions on several occasions, leading me to the conclusion that I was 100 percent human, and much to my surprise, I was psychologically *normal*. I certainly did not feel this way, however. In all honesty, my emotional range had only fluctuated between happiness and occasional irritation with a hint of anger prior to my mom's death. My emotional state in June 2013 unsettled me and revealed emotional depths that I had never known before.

On most days, I was a self-described "walking zombie," soaking in the essentials in order to make it through each painstaking moment. My basic goal was to experience each day without any major emotional foibles, steer clear of potential conflict, and perfect my escape route across situations and settings. This basically resulted in my experiencing social and emotional isolation in most situations. With the exception of raw and emotional flare-ups, my senses were dulled to virtually everything around me.

> My basic goal was to experience each day without any major emotional foibles, steer clear of potential conflict, and perfect my escape plan across settings.

My hotel outing awakened my senses, at least to some degree. As the raindrops pounded against my skin, I felt a surge of energy. Each raindrop was a God-breathed message that I was, in fact, alive. Each one was a syllable in the formation of words from God that I desperately needed to hear. *I am here with you. I hear your cry. You are not alone.* The rain jolted me awake to the reality that I was in tremendous pain. It caused me to recognize the depth of my sorrow. Drop by drop, I realized how disconnected I was from myself and others. At the same time, the rain offered amazing consolation, which I anxiously craved. The rain masked the tears I had tirelessly shed since my mom's death, providing me with a small window of normalcy. It was as if God were crying along with me, shedding months of emotional pain and devastation in one evening. It was not until I returned to the hotel room that I was able to see myself face-to-face in the mirror. *I was a complete mess!*

###

July 2, 2013

Today wasn't a good day at all! After a negative experience at work, I ended up cycling into a crying spell, one that manifested itself at my first grief support group meeting and beyond. I lashed out at Stanley, resulting in us getting into a verbal scuffle. However, once I calmed down, we were able to smooth things out. He even stayed on the telephone with me until 3:00 a.m., all the while, I was snot-faced and crying. Now I'm sitting in my bed, about to make an attempt to sleep through the night. Please, Lord, let Your child rest! This "not sleeping" is taking a major toll on my life!

Consistent with the previous month's theme, July 2013 proved to be equally challenging on all fronts. It was becoming more and more difficult for me to mask the pain I was experiencing, as additional stressors mounted in other areas of my life. I had always felt a sense of protection within the work environment, as if God had shielded me from typical work-related shenanigans over the years. Nevertheless, just as God had shifted so many things in my life leading up to July 2013, He was preparing me for the same at work. *Boy, was I not ready!*

Work had become a safe haven for me following my mom's death, related in large part to its predictability and relatively easy rhythm. I received my courses, I prepared to teach them, and I taught them with excellence. I attended meetings, and I engaged with my coworkers in an appropriate and professional manner. I advised students and offered mentorship to those who expressed interest. I had always received positive remarks across semesters via student evaluations. Further, my faculty evaluations had always been stellar across domains. *So why had I been reprimanded for a minor issue when my work history reflected excellent performance?*

I felt angry and overwhelmed, yet recognized my inability to fully express my thoughts and feelings with my supervisor. So I swallowed my already bottled-up feelings and carried them with me to a grief support group meeting after work. Amy had recommended that I consider participating in a support group, and after thinking about it, I decided that it may help me cope. Further, I had not been meeting with her and recognized the need for some type of external support.

> I swallowed my already bottled-up feelings and carried them with me to a grief support group meeting after work.

What better place to release my feelings surrounding my mom's death? I would be surrounded by others walking a similar journey. Little did I know that an innocent charge to tell the group about myself would result in an emotional breakdown and tear fest! *I was so humiliated*, yet I stayed for the remainder of the group meeting, if only to avoid additional stares. As soon as the meeting concluded, I remember racing to my car, vowing never to return again—at least not to that group!

Given that my group meeting did not go as well as I had hoped, I reached out to my brother via telephone, hoping for a listening ear and kind words. While I do not recall the specifics of the conversation, I do remember my brother sharing that he felt as if I were replacing our mom with him. He stated that he felt overwhelmed by the thought of being there for me constantly. And that was all it took that night! Once again, I verbally lashed out in anger. This time, however, I was able to regain my composure in the moment and communicate my feelings in a more constructive manner. *It was progress!* Of course, the energy I had expended in the conversation with my brother resulted in additional emotional fatigue, which in my case meant more crying after the fact.

Crying, unfortunately, made it more difficult for me to go to bed. Sleep continued to escape me, which I resented more and more. With all of the energy I had spent just getting through each day, one would think that sleep would be easy for me to achieve! But, no–the more I pursued sleep, the more it ran away from me! After seven months of sleepless nights, I recognized the danger to my mind, body, and spirit, yet carried on as if everything were normal.

###

August 2, 2013

11:30 a.m. I'm enjoying myself under a palm tree, looking out at the water on Waikiki Beach. I woke up and went for a two-mile run earlier along the beach. I'm loving this day and this entire experience so far! It's been easy to feel connected to God here, given the amazing scenery everywhere. I've also recognized the beauty of simply being with no particular aim. The sufficiency of God's grace is with me in each moment. I've thought about Mama a lot, and each time, I silently pray for the grace of God to carry and strengthen me.

Summer 2013 was, by far, the worst summer of my life! And after experiencing the majority of it at this point, I understood that the only way to "do grief" was to *do grief* head-on! I understood that there would be no racing through it or bypassing its stronghold. *I despised that, in all honesty!* The interesting paradox during this season was that I had counseled so many children and families who had previously been at this same juncture in their lives. I had encouraged them to "walk into the fire" of grief, embrace its complexities, and interact with it without self-judgment. It seemed comical to find this *wisdom* helpful or even necessary, yet I knew it was the only way.

Wow! Amy's words still resonated in my mind, nearly three months after she had spoken them! *Relax into the pain, relax into the pain.* Shockingly (to myself anyway), I kept my promise to God and resumed therapy with Amy in August 2013, almost three months after I had suspended meeting with her. By the grace of God, she welcomed me back into her office with open arms, as well as an open mind. Plain and simple, I had to *do* grief, or *it* would certainly consume me!

God offered me a reference point from my work as a psychologist. *He reminded me of the times that I had worked with children who feared needle injections of all things!* As I sat beside wailing children and their overwhelmed parents, I had engaged them in breathing exercises. I had modeled deep inhalations and tempered exhalations, all the while explaining that one of the worst things to do in the face of physical pain was to hold your breath. Rather, I encouraged hearty exhales, noting their impact on the mind and body, in terms of relaxation. As counterintuitive as it seemed, I explained how relaxing just prior to the needle injection would actually reduce the pain experienced in the moment.

It suddenly became clear to me what Amy had tried to say to me prior to the summer. *I needed to relax into the pain of my experience in order to feel better, heal, and grow. Maintaining a plan of escape would only serve to prolong the devastation of it all.*

> Plain and simple, I had to *do* grief, or *it* would certainly consume me!

In His infinite wisdom and planning, the Lord planned a wonderful trip for me to begin what I refer to as my "fire walk." He orchestrated a sequence of events that would afford me a space to fully relax into my pain, beginning with a trip to Honolulu, Hawaii. Of course, this was unbeknownst to me. Had God informed me that a weeklong work/pleasure trip to Hawaii would be the backdrop for His unfolding plan, *I might have cancelled the trip!*

Now as a gentleman, He did not just throw me into the fire! No, He gradually and carefully captivated me with His presence, impressing me with His beautiful creations in the form of gorgeous sunsets and lingering rainbows, over the course of the first few days in Hawaii. Each day that I walked along the beach, snorkeled, or watched whales, God drew me closer and closer to Him by reminding me just how big He is! He comforted me time and time again in the evenings, as I sat on my hotel balcony, prayed, and read His Word. Finally, He graced me with notable improvements in my sleep, for the first time since my mom died. It was a glorious courtship, one that I desperately craved as I awoke each morning. I felt loved and seen by, as well as connected to, Him.

On the fourth day in Hawaii, however, I felt the Lord impress upon me through prayer, the need to be honest about and expressive of my feelings beyond the purviews of my journal. *I was absolutely mortified. Angry, to be more precise!* How could God expect me to be so open about my private feelings? Didn't He understand that my mom had just died *only eight months ago*? Didn't He appreciate that I was already wrestling with so much in my heart, mind, body, and spirit? Couldn't He understand how difficult this would be for me? Why had He courted me so well in the days leading up to this point, only to turn His back?

God's definition of relaxing into the pain was my opening up about what had been so well hidden since my mom's death—*my feelings*. His idea of relaxing was unearthing feelings of sadness, anger, frustration, as well as struggles with intimacy that I had never confronted before. Grieving the death of my mom had simply been the *catalyst* for unveiling so much of my emotional undercurrent.

I sought God's counsel regarding how to navigate my new *relaxed* state, and He provided a unique opportunity for me to relax … at the altar of a small Hawaiian church! *Yes, that's right!* Who knew that I would share my deepest pains with barefoot Hawaiian strangers on a Sunday morning? God knew. *He also knew that I was finally ready to relax into the pain of it all.*

"When you go through deep waters, I will be with you. When you go through rivers of difficulty, you will not drown. When you walk through the fire of oppression, you will not be burned up; the flames will not consume you" (Isaiah 43:2 NLT). I would not drown. *I would not be burned up. I would not be consumed. Isaiah 43:2 became my anthem from that day forward.*

###

September 30, 2013

10:00 p.m. I just returned home from my first church small group meeting (as a participant). It was quite interesting! Six folks participated, including me. It was a mixed crowd, ethnically, socioeconomically, and emotionally. Tonight, we introduced ourselves and identified some personal prayer needs. I identified the need for more openness and vulnerability with others. Ha! *This is the theme of my existence right now!* I'm thrilled that I so openly exposed my need … with total strangers! I shared about Mama's death, as well as my control issues. I'd say that I opened myself up pretty well for a first group. *I just feel in my spirit that I must do this!*

Hawaii had been the practice ground for what God was leading me to do throughout the fall 2013. I had feared stepping out of my emotional comfort zone and into the spotlight in August; yet, here I was at the end of September sharing my emotional and spiritual needs with people who I did not even know. I knew this was a step in the right direction, and thankfully, both my tears and expressions of need were met with compassion and understanding.

What was interesting about the church small group was how different everyone seemed to be. I was the youngest person in the group, the oldest people well into their sixties. The theme of the group was singlehood, which seemed to be the only thing we all had in common. I recall leaving the first meeting a bit frustrated, asking the Lord about what could possibly come from such a diverse group of churchgoers and how people so seemingly different than me could understand what I was experiencing along my grief journey.

God offered no reply to my inquiry, but gently challenged me to keep my mind and heart open to what He would do in and through me as part of this unique group. I knew that I had no control whatsoever, so I readily accepted his challenge to return to the group the following week. At this point, I had foregone participating in the original grief support group. Following the first debacle in July, I attended another support meeting at a local church for a short stint, only to be met with individuals I deemed severely depressed. Week after week, there seemed to be no movement in the themes discussed or strategies offered to cope with the grief journey. The constant repetition of storytelling without a quest for personal understanding or growth felt incredibly burdensome, and I knew that I did not want my grief experience to be one riddled with stagnation.

While I certainly had a story to tell, I was determined not to *become* my story. It reminded me of testimonies I had heard at church over the years, where people wore their stories as a badge of honor ... not for the sake of God receiving the glory, but simply as a tool to feel relevant, seen, or heard. Perhaps judgmental, but I sensed my need to seek counsel from those who were dedicated Christ followers—those who embodied hope—as opposed to those in the group who seemingly wanted to remain emotionally disoriented and wedded to their grief-stricken narratives. Regardless of the depths of my pain, my hope remained in the living God, and I did not want to sink any further into my emotional well.

> I had a story to tell, but I was determined not to *become* my story.

If anything, individuals within the church small group would see and interact with me at least weekly, which I thought might offer a sense of community in a place where I had none. While not overly optimistic about His plan, I had no choice but to continue down the path that God was preparing for me. He had said to go through the deep waters and step into the rivers of difficulty. So, I simply obeyed. Isaiah 43:2.

###

October 1, 2013

So my daily devotional discussed the benefit of affliction (Psalm 119:71). One of the lines that struck me in particular was, "Till the storms and vicissitudes of God's providence beat upon him again and again, his character appears marred and clouded. But, trials clear away the obscurity, perfect the outlines of his disposition, and give brightness and blessing to his life."

And it's so true! I've seen this year how life's storms have brought me to a place of awareness, acknowledgment, and greater acceptance of who I am. I've also experienced God in amazing ways! It's like He's pouring out His love and calling me closer to Him. *I love this relationship!* It feels great to be loved, cared for, and pursued by Jesus, the perfect gentleman!

So tonight, I was scrolling through a social media site and stumbled upon Psalm 107:23-24, which says, "Some went out on the sea in ships; they were merchants on the mighty waters. They saw the works of the Lord, His wonderful deeds in the deep." That's where I feel like I am—in the deep—*and I believe God is calling me deeper even still.*

The *benefit* of affliction—what a paradoxical phrase! By October, I had begun to view grief as a necessary tool–one that I did not enjoy by any means, but one that I knew represented so much more than what I could see on the surface. Psalm 119:71 (NLT) reads, "My suffering was good for me, for it taught me to pay attention to your decrees." Oh, yes, the Lord had *certainly* caught my attention over the past eleven months! I was definitely more attuned to His presence, as well as His Word.

Prior to my mom's death, I had not ever experienced suffering in its fullness. Yes, I had experienced setbacks, physical challenges, and relational hardships throughout my life. *But* actual *suffering?* No, it had not yet knocked on my life's door. I had not yet experienced suffering's vice grip in any area of my life. Looking back, I can acknowledge that I lived a life filled primarily with mountaintop experiences, from my education and career to core friendships to my health. I took my life for granted, expecting the doors that I knocked on to be opened and the windows that

I peered into to titillate my senses. God's love and grace had afforded me amazing luxuries across time and space.

> I took my life for granted, expecting the doors that I knocked on to be opened and the windows that I peered into to titillate my senses.

Of course, the Father wanted me to experience the finer things in life, as any parent would. Yet, like any parent, He also wanted me to approach life with perspective, not just through rose-colored lenses. This season had led me to reevaluate God and His ways, which I knew I would never fully understand. Yet, I sensed that God planned to use my mom's death to benefit me and others—*the benefit of affliction*. I had no idea how He would do this, but I knew that He was faithful and cared for me. *My experience in Hawaii had taught me that!*

October 8, 2013

I'm reviewing the message from church on Sunday, which dealt with Jesus asking the disciples to "come and see" when they asked where Jesus was staying. I feel like God is telling me the same thing. "Mekel, come and see for yourself what's in store. Come and see. Just follow me, and trust me." The pastor shared a visual of a person kneeling before God, humbling himself in full worship as a response to God's leading. That's how I feel—so wide open. I've never felt this receptive to God's direction. I have no idea where I'm going. But each day I just get up and go and see.

God continued to press into me at every turn, at this point challenging me to draw nearer to Him by stepping out into the unknown. It was one thing to trust God in Hawaii when I was surrounded by beautiful sunsets, rainbows, and fresh air. I could see His hand in full view, as He guided me along the sunny path! It was an entirely different course of action to take a step into what I perceived as dark and unknown territory. Imagine playing the game hide-and-seek for a moment. You close your eyes and count to ten and then race to find your hidden friends. As you peer into closets and look under beds to find them, you do so with a bit of reservation. You know your friends are hiding, and you know you will eventually find them. Yet you have no idea whether your pursuit of them will result in your own scare.

In some ways, this is how I felt about God's charge to "come and see." Would my pursuit be met with something worse than my current state? Each morning, however, I woke up and accepted His daily challenge, with both excitement and fear in my heart. I wanted to believe that as I tasted God's offerings, He would prove that He was, indeed, good. God had confirmed His loving nature in Hawaii, so I trusted that He would not harm me in any way. At the same time, so many what-if questions bombarded my mind all at once. *What if* I did not like what I saw after I followed His instructions? *What if*, upon my arrival, I had no idea about how to return to my original dwelling? *What if* God's comedic side was at play and nothing was there after all?

Yet, I considered my options. If I decided to return to the place I had been, I would be miserable. I could *not* return to the emotional, physical, or spiritual state I had been in throughout the prior months. I knew this would only result in more depression and deeper emotional plummeting. If I decided to stay in the place I currently resided, I would be just as stagnant as the people I had interacted with in the grief support group. So I had no option but to move forward, following and trusting Jesus in the midst of the unknown, and He met me every step of the way. Little by little, I realized that His hands were outstretched toward me, guiding me all the while. *And much to my surprise, each step did not lead to darkness but rather more light.*

> Each morning, I woke up and accepted His daily challenge, with both excitement and fear in my heart.

It dawned on me throughout the fall that God was an active God. *Think about it!* In twenty-four hours, God paints the sky a thousand times over, breathes life into so many souls, and creates places of refuge for those in greatest need. *Only an active and creative God could accomplish all of that!* I realized that, perhaps, one of the reasons for the frequent shifting tides in my life was that God did not *want* me to stay in the same place. He knew that I was grieving, and I believe He recognized the value of my grieving. *Yet I knew that while grief as a whole was ever-changing across the lifespan, its firm grip on every area of my life was seasonal.* Ecclesiastes 3:1–4 (ESV) reads, "For everything there is a season, and a time for every matter under heaven: a time to be born, and a time to die; a time to plant, and a time to pluck up what is planted; a time to kill, and a time to heal; a time to break down, and a time to build up; a time to weep, and a time to laugh; *a time to mourn*, and a time to dance."

Perhaps the Lord knew that if I were left to my own devices, I might shrink into my comfort zone and be consumed by the emotional quicksand I was standing in. Perhaps He knew that my time to mourn might overwhelm my time to live in the fullness of His loving splendor and grace. The more I considered God's requests, the more I embraced His concern for me. *What loving father would leave his child in a state of emotional pain or paralysis, after all?* Of course, I could not stay where I had been! It was time to pick up my pallet and walk ... *again!*

November 28, 2013

Thanksgiving Day 2013. I woke up, shopped for my holiday goodies, went to the gym, and even took a power nap. Then I spent the evening with one of the women from my church small group and her family. I had such a nice time and felt very welcomed. Nevertheless, I miss Mama. This was the first Thanksgiving holiday without her. Last year, as we left our family's house, Mama said it would be her last Thanksgiving. I wish I could hear her voice today, if only for a moment. Even if I wasn't able to see her, we definitely would have talked today if she were alive. She truly loved all of me! I know she's living it up in heaven, laughing and relaxing. I know she'd be proud of me.

Thanksgiving 2012, my mom's last Thanksgiving on earth, was filled will lots of laughter, food, and fellowship with family. She enjoyed the moments with old and new friends and celebrated memories from the past. She knew that her life's clock was rapidly ticking, and she courageously shared this with our family. On the drive home from the Thanksgiving festivities, she reminded my brother and me that the holiday was, indeed, her last and then proceeded to discuss her wishes for her memorial service, yet again.

Neither my brother nor I knew what our first Thanksgiving without our mom would feel like. We discussed my flying to Texas to spend the holiday with our family, yet I felt the need to remain in California … if only to prove to myself that I could emotionally survive the holiday. Something inside of me knew that I needed to expand my coping repertoire beyond my comfort zones in Texas. Amy and I had spent countless hours throughout the fall identifying support systems in California, and spending time with one of my new friends from church was necessary. I needed to take another step in the right direction, thereby expanding my intimacy circle.

Intimacy—this word had become my constant companion across time. Nearly one year after my mom's death, I opened the door for close connection, and this frightened me. *Would she be able to support me in the midst of my grief? If she saw my raw and broken moments, would she still be there for me? How would she handle my tears and expressions of loneliness?* Nevertheless, the beautiful paradox of fear is that it simultaneously restrains and propels you. I recall driving to my new friend's family's home, sitting outside in my car, and contemplating whether I would actually make the trek across the street, walk up the stairwell to the front door, and cross over the threshold into the house. I knew the answer was yes, in large part because of the bowl of banana pudding seated on my passenger seat. I had promised to bring a dessert to the gathering, and warm pudding was just not acceptable.

Relaxing Into the Pain

> The beautiful paradox of fear is that it simultaneously restrains and propels you.

So I picked up my bowl of pudding and headed for the front door, which was red and seemed enormous at the time. In true God fashion, I was not greeted by my friend (which made me more nervous). Rather, I was welcomed by her daughter-in-law. She hugged me and invited me in, after which I met several other strangers who welcomed me with their hugs and pleasantries. Though I scanned the crowd, my friend was nowhere to be found—well, at least for the first thirty to sixty seconds, which felt like a lifetime. As I made my way into the backyard, I finally exchanged eye contact, smiles, and hugs with my friend from church. *Did I mention God's sense of humor?* More than nine hours later, I was laughing and playing games with her family, as if I had been a part of their family for years! I had not laughed that much since my mom had died, and it made me feel alive and whole. Around 10:30 p.m., I finally left the gathering because of the time (not because of enjoyment). I drove home, content and proud of myself for walking through God's open door—a big red door, *a door of hope.*

###

December 29, 2013

I'm watching a documentary about a man who confronted his past sins and admitted them to his family members, who he had hurt tremendously. This reminds me of my own journey throughout 2013 in therapy. Entering the therapy space and sharing all of the dark pieces of myself with Amy was one of the most difficult days of my life! Yet now, I'm free! I'm so ready to enter 2014 with no bondages. I've released a lot of prior issues that have held me back for decades. I've confronted my flaws and have courageously begun the process of working on them. I've practiced how to resolve conflict in relationships. And my relationship with God is constant and deeper than it's ever been. I just *know* that I've been preparing for something magical in 2014! *Oh, I can't wait to see what unfolds in the coming days!*

All things had worked together for my good, according to God's purpose, throughout the fall. I felt assured of His goodness and maintained an enthusiasm about where He might lead me in the days to come. It had been a long time coming, but I finally felt hopeful–not a fleeting sense of hope, but an enduring kind. December 2013 signaled the one-year mark of my grief race, and I could honestly say that I was generally pacing myself through it all. Well, God was helping me keep pace.

Well-intentioned people had said that I would be in shock throughout the first year and that the second year would be riddled with emotional ups and downs. I had heard every spiritual euphemism and comforting Scripture one could think of, and at times, I became overwhelmed by the barrage of "helpful" chatter around me. At this point, if I had heard someone say, "You're going to feel [insert feeling]," one more time, I think I would have exploded. Year one had neither been a textbook version of grief nor a parallel of others' experiences along the grief journey.

God had prepared this race—*my race*—specifically for *me*, and no one could predict its trajectory.

> Year one had neither been a textbook version of grief nor a parallel of others' experiences with grief.

Therefore, since we are surrounded by such a great cloud of witnesses, let us throw off everything that hinders and the sin that so easily entangles. And, let us run with perseverance the race marked out for us, fixing our eyes on Jesus, the pioneer and perfecter of faith. For the joy set before Him, He endured the cross, scorning its shame, and sat down at the right hand of the throne of God. Consider Him who endured such opposition from sinners, so that you will not grow weary and lose heart. (Hebrews 12:1–3 NIV)

This Scripture had become my new life verse, particularly as I considered how God was calling me to "throw off everything" that had hindered me up to this point in my life.

Again, I experienced God as *constantly* in motion. *Did He ever rest?* He had not called me to casually toss out the emotional and spiritual issues that held me hostage over the years, though this may have felt more comfortable throughout the year. No, He required active faith and works on my end! God had so much in store for me, and I was excited to see what lied ahead! I knew that it would not be easy. Jesus Himself *endured*—He sustained and tolerated—the cross. Yet, He sat down at the right hand of the throne of God. *This is where I wanted to reside!* I imagined what it would be like to sit next to my Abba Father, like a little girl next to her daddy, looking up to Him in love and adoration.

So I knew that I had to continue running my race, consistently and with endurance, so that I might not lose heart.

###

February 4, 2014

So, umm, yeah … I'm in San Francisco right now. It's 7:22 a.m., and I just woke up. Super long and frustrating story short. I, me, Mekel completely overlooked the fact that a visa is necessary to travel to India. I'm scheduled to present there at an international children's palliative care conference and overlooked this *minor* point. Well, it dawned on me on Sunday night, which resulted in my racing to San Francisco, the location where the Indian consulate is. Lord, have mercy! Yesterday was filled with frustration and anger (with myself), as well as tears—plenty of tears! My conversation with God consisted of … well, silence, as I was too frustrated to even pray. Sad, but true! My faith waned, and I felt utterly hopeless. Yes, this sucks for a mature Christian! The situation was stacked against me in every way—no appointment and a random walk-in, an incomplete application packet, and interactions with people whose vocabulary was limited to saying, "No, I can't help you!"

Nevertheless (and despite my lack of prayer and limited faith), God shifted the atmosphere. I interacted with a woman who extended some grace regarding my situation, and then I spoke with a manager who let me process some of the application. At the end of the day, I wasn't able to submit the packet, yet I was provided hope in the fact that I could return today, submit an application for an urgent visa, and pick it up by the end of the day.

So it's now 7:44 a.m., and I'm waiting outside of the building, which opens at 9:00 a.m. However, I'll be standing outside at 8:30 a.m., waiting for the doors to open and be the very first person in line!

My question to myself is this: "Where is your faith, Mekel?" The answer is, "I have no idea!" I was caught up in a cycle of lack of sleep, minor irritations, and the thought of losing thousands of dollars on this trip. And my faith exited stage left! I'm not pleased with this recognition. I could say, "I'm only human," though that seems only fitting as a lame excuse for not exercising spiritual warfare. I think a more accurate description of my current state is this: "I am broken and in desperate need of God's moment-by-moment grace and love." A series of daily hassles, coupled with the threat of not capitalizing on something I've worked so hard for, broke me. It literally broke me … after all of my Sunday sermons, individual time with God, prayer, and songs. I am no better. I'm at square one. I'm broken!

Today, instead of beating myself up about not being the spiritual superhero for the day, I'm simply going to celebrate that God is with me no matter what. He loves me no matter what. He "gets me" at all times. And He enjoys that I desperately need Him. Heck, isn't that what the Christian faith walk is all about? Total dependence on God! Praise God for a new day! It's 7:53 a.m. now. Just a few more moments.

"Sufferings are God's winds, His contrary winds, sometimes His strong winds. They are God's hurricanes, but, they take human life and lift it to higher levels and towards God's heavens." This is *so* relevant to my experiences over the past week. I don't want to abuse or misrepresent suffering, particularly as I see this applicable to the most catastrophic of events. Yet, the hassles, hurts, and inconveniences I felt this week appeared to be strong winds. Perhaps I only felt the winds because my feet weren't firmly planted on the ground. Perhaps the winds were a reminder of my moment-by-moment dependence on God. Perhaps the winds are a glimpse into the true winds that God is preparing me for. I don't know. But I *do* know that I am a total wreck without God's strength! Yesterday, I was leaning on my own strength and nearly fell apart. The lightest winds caused my body to sway and emotionally unravel! Yes, I need God in my life. He's my anchor in all things!

Looking back on this moment in my life, it seems almost comical that I did not even consider the need to check whether a visa was necessary for an international trip! It was not as if I had not traveled internationally before! However, I know it was less of an intellectual misstep and more of an emotional overload. My internal hard drive had reached its limit, and I simply forgot something that mattered. It was not the first time this had happened since my mom's death. As I sat in my car, I reflected upon the bills that had simply been overlooked in the preceding months, the telephone calls that had not been returned, and the long-forgotten items on my to-do list at work.

After a relatively uneventful fall semester and continued efforts to run the race God designed for me, I truly believe this moment was simply an overflow of the emotional security that I had been trying to cling to after my intimate experience with Jesus in Hawaii. It is interesting to me that after clearly experiencing the magnitude of God's presence and allowing Him to take over the role of captain in my life, *I still wanted to be in control of my own emotional, physical, and spiritual journey. Why could I not let go and trust God?*

I believe that my forgetfulness was a symptom of my lingering desire to be in control. It was a reflection of my need to chart my own course without God's help. I had experienced intermittent moments of surrender with God since summer 2013, yet I still clung to my own "enough-ness." Thankfully, God showered me with His grace that day, affording me connection with a slew of strangers who felt pity on me. Yet I think He also allowed this memory lapse in order for me to fall on my knees *yet again* in total surrender to Him. And it worked! He boxed me into a space where I could no longer move. I had literally raced across the state of California, doing all that I could do in my own strength to "make things happen." But I could not *do* anything to fix the situation. I could no longer speak even. Despite years of church service, individual prayer and meditation, and even church retreats, I had no eloquent prayers or thoughtful reflections to share. All I had were heartfelt tears, the kind that burn as they slowly and stingingly roll down your cheeks. I also had the recognition that I was broken and needed God's help.

That day was a breakthrough of sorts—not only in terms of my expressed need for God but also in my shifting into a place of self-forgiveness. As a self-proclaimed high-achiever and perfectionist doer, my standards were high, and minimal room was afforded for personal error of any kind. Nevertheless, on that day, I decided to simply *be* without any pressure placed on myself. I made the choice to shift the focus from my inadequacies to God's grace, love, and pure understanding of me. I do not think I had ever done that before! *God's winds were shifting, and my foundation was cracking all the while.*

I realized that *with reconstruction comes destruction* … of old ways of thinking, of negative attitudes, and of unhealthy patterns of behavior. God was reconstructing me into a more solid frame. My mom's death had only offered the first blow to my shaky foundation, and everything that had transpired since her death provided the continual drilling necessary to uncover my deepest hurts and fears. Imagine this for a moment. With drilling comes vibration on all sides, shakiness, loose footing, and uncertainty. This was God's plan for me throughout this time—to literally shake me up—all for the purpose of refashioning me in His wonderful image.

> I realized that *with reconstruction comes destruction* … of old ways of thinking, of negative attitudes, and of unhealthy patterns of behavior.

I knew that God was with me and that He cared for me. That's all that seemed to matter at that moment.

###

February 13, 2014

Well, this time has finally come—my last moments in Mumbai, India. It's hard to believe that a week has gone by! And what a wonderful week it's been!

Today, I woke up, ate breakfast at the hotel, and then headed out to explore the streets of Mumbai. I walked around my hotel and surrounding area and then took a taxi to Mahim Station. I needed to head there anyway in order to meet up with a tour company later in the day. The taxi ride was about forty minutes because of traffic. Then I started out on foot in the Mahim Station area. It was quite interesting!

I was encountered by a group of young children who begged me for food and money. I smiled. They smiled, and I ended up giving them the equivalent of about $2.50. Probably not the best move but an act of kindness nonetheless. I continued my journey and stumbled upon a cow and goat in the midst of traffic. Later I learned that they would be sacrificed as part of traditional religious practice in India. After roaming for a bit, I searched for a local Christian church and found it. I'd brought a prayer floral necklace with me to hang at the altar in Mama's memory.

So I sat, prayed, and reflected upon the day's experiences. I prayed to the Lord for blessing me with a wonderful mother. I cried tears of sadness about missing Mama, followed by tears of joy in thankfulness to the Lord for all He is in my life. And I disconnected for a moment from all of the noise. One of the most remarkable moments was observing a young woman walk on her knees from the back of the church all the way down the center aisle on her way to the altar. She stopped every so often to pray and then continued on the path. When she reached the altar, she lingered there in prayer for a while. It was so beautiful to observe! Watching her reminded me of the need to truly revere God. Her act of walking on her knees symbolized full surrender, full submission, and pure reverence toward God. Wow! It was very awe-inspiring!

I'd like to begin praying with more surrender to the Lord, and I'll need to pray about how to best do this when I'm back at home. I feel so connected to God and don't want to lose this experience.

Actually, I don't want to lose *any* of it. I pray that I am changed forever as a result of this trip.

God allowed me to witness the beauty of *full surrender,* in the form of a woman kneeling her way to the altar. Even reflecting upon that moment in time is emotional and awe-inspiring! How often do we actually bow down to the Lord, revere Him and His presence, and honor Him with our actions? I can say that while I strive to be this type of Christian in my heart, I fail daily! In that moment, I recall thinking how physically taxing it must have been for her to seek after God in this way. One to two minutes of kneeling during physical exercise strained my knees, giving way to aches and pains. I couldn't imagine how she endured this level of strain.

Pick up your mat and walk. Walk in the face of difficulty. Walk on your knees if you have to. Crawl if need be. Do not focus on how tired you are. Just walk. Focus on who I am and what I have done for you. *Walk.* These are the thoughts that reigned in my spirit on my last day in India. God had allowed me to travel all the way around the world to speak this simple, yet profound, message to my heart. *Walk—that was my charge!*

I had complained throughout my experience in Hawaii, questioning God's awareness of my inward pain. I had embraced an understanding of what it meant to relax into the pain of my mom's death, as well as other internal revelations. I had begun to walk, yet I continued to challenge God with each step. I desperately wanted freedom, but I was tired. So in His infinite wisdom, the Lord provided a glimpse into what it looks like to wholeheartedly surrender in the midst of discomfort. My question: "How often do we actually bow down to the Lord, revere Him and His presence, and honor Him with our actions?" resonated within me.

Just as He had done in Hawaii, God allowed me to experience amazing emotional heights, as well as glimpses into His goodness in India. In Hawaii, this had occurred primarily through observation of His beautiful creation. I peered into His goodness as a bystander and took a step of faith at the altar. In India, however, God afforded me a peek into another human being's experience, a living example of what surrender looked like. *And oh, how beautiful it was!*

###

February 28, 2014

Today was very low key and quiet. I stayed home all day with the exception of a fifteen-minute outing to Whole Foods to pick up some snacks. I watched a lot of TV since my cable was installed today at my new loft apartment. And I barely spoke. Honestly, it was nice to be quiet all day.

So now, it's about 10:00 p.m., and I'm heading to bed. All I have tomorrow is a 1:00 p.m. private practice patient. Quiet day. I may hang out with a few girls from church, though I'm not sure. It all depends on how I feel throughout the day tomorrow. Today, I even canceled an outing with a guy I met recently. I just wasn't in the mood to be out, coupled with today's rainy weather, fatigue, and a whopping (and crusty) fever blister on my lower lip! *Great!*

Anyway, I have tried not to focus on the stress I've felt the past few days. I didn't spend any dedicated time in my Bible, but

I did reflect on some devotionals and thoughts I encountered throughout the day. My aim is to simply be me, hold my head up, and continue working hard and excelling like I always do! This is a battle I cannot fix, so God will have to take care of this, lead me, and lift me when needed. That's the plan, plain and simple!

I sure wish I could talk to Mama! I still haven't encountered her in an audible way. I've stopped praying for her to show up in my dreams. I'm not sure if that really matters! So again, I simply wait and see how this plays out as well. That seems to be my life's theme right now. *Wait. Watch. Surrender.*

Perhaps that's the point of all of this—to remind me to surrender control over to the Lord and fully trust Him. Well, I have no choice but to do so in the midst of this witch hunt! I can do nothing! It feels as if I'm watching the scenario play out with me on the sidelines, almost in slow motion! It's surreal!

For now, I rest. That's all I can do today. Again, I pray for peaceful and undisturbed slumber.

Wait, watch, and surrender—the three words that epitomized my experience. This was the first time that I felt emotionally and spiritually relaxed since my mom's death. My natural instinct to *do* something was completely overridden by God's plan for me to simply *be*. His supernatural excavation project was in full swing, and even I could not deny the growth that had occurred within me. One of the most beautiful things that one can experience in life is observing personal growth, particularly in an area that has created so much internal tension. For me, that tension resulted in anger because of my inability to feel in control. I had not wanted to relinquish control following my mom's death. I had not wanted to fully surrender to God's plan throughout my grief journey. I had not yet known what it was like to trust wholeheartedly, without reservation. *Yet, I found myself finally admitting that I was not enough.* I can imagine that God celebrated wildly on this day! After so many midcourse corrections, intense spiritual reconstruction, and ongoing showers of grace, His child had finally come to the realization that she could not travel along life's road alone. Around this time, I also experienced a challenging work-related event, one that exhausted me mentally, emotionally, and physically. This, mind you, was on the heels of my beginning to experience a sense of emotional relief. And as I look back at the experience now, I can see that it was yet another challenge from God to me to rely on Him. The circumstances at work were completely out of my control, and I chose to stand firm, as opposed to emotionally react. *God was surely pleased!*

Truth be told, I was pleased with myself! After so many months of self-judgment and self-criticism regarding my behaviors following my mom's death, I felt proud of my ability to emotionally manage the stressors before me. Was I 100 percent in control of my emotions at all times? *Absolutely not!* Nevertheless, I was intentional daily about waiting for God, watching for His will to be revealed, and surrendering to the things that I could not control. Amy and I continued to meet weekly, and I began to value my time with her in a different way.

> After so many midcourse corrections, intense spiritual reconstruction, and ongoing showers of grace, His child had finally come to the realization that she could not travel along life's road alone.

It had been almost fifteen months since my mom's death, and while I longed for her presence, my understanding of her death was clearer. The Lord had begun to piece together many aspects of my inner self that I had not previously known, and as these connections were made, I felt stronger. My reliance on God increased, and my intimacy with Him deepened with each passing day. *After so many months, the dark and weighty veil had finally lifted.*

###

March 3, 2014

It's Monday morning, and I just got on the train to work. Today should be a quiet day. I have a joint interview with a prospective student at 10:00 a.m., followed by a couple of student meetings.

Isaiah 61 – I'm reflecting on this Scripture from yesterday's message at church. Isaiah saw and heard the Lord for the first time after King Uzziah died. It took his death to open Isaiah's spiritual eyes and ears. This alone reminded me of Mama's death. Though I desperately wish she were here, I know that Mama was a counterfeit God in my life. In a crazy, cosmic way, her death forced me to seek God more and more earnestly. In the middle of the night (and day), I know that I can't pick up the phone and call Mama, my problem solver for thirty-seven years! I'm *forced* to go to God and work things out with Him. And for this, I'm thankful (in a weird way) to the Lord for Mama's death. *Crazy!*

Then Isaiah 61 says that Isaiah learned of his frailties, his insecurities, and his brokenness. He realized the deepest parts of himself and had to simply sit with it, after which God asked who would be willing and able to serve. Isaiah spoke up and said, "Me, me, me!"

Isaiah's story could not have rung more true in my spirit. The parallels between his experiences following King Uzziah's death and my experiences following my mom's death were exquisitely similar! Like Isaiah, my eyes were opened to the truth of who I was as a result of my mom's death.

While living, my mom was my reliable sounding board. When I considered new employment opportunities, I called my mom to weigh in. Prior to moving to a new place of residence, I consulted her. I conferred with her, almost daily about dating and relationship issues. She and I discussed my friendships, as well as relationships with family members. I deferred to her judgment about concerns related to my move to California. I sought her advice related to teaching and advising my students. My mom served as my counsel throughout every aspect of my young and adult life! I listened attentively to hear her thoughts, frequently relying upon her opinions to make decisions. *For all intents and purposes, my mom was my god!*

Of course, I never thought of her in this way prior to her death. I was the daughter who needed counsel, and she was my motherly counselor. The Great Counselor, Jesus, played second fiddle to my mom, unbeknownst to me on a conscious level. Yes, I pursued Him and sought His counsel as well; however, this was typically *after* I had consulted with my mom! She was my living Bible, and I soaked in every truth that she spoke. God's Word served as a reference guide to my mom's numerous parables.

> She was my living Bible, and I soaked in every truth that she spoke.

While this, indeed, contained all of the ingredients for a loving mother-daughter relationship, it also prevented me from being a woman after God's heart! In retrospect, I can see that my relationship with my mom was the focal point of my life. *Imagine being seated behind someone during a concert.* You can see and appreciate the stage, but the head of the person in front of you occasionally blocks your view throughout the performance. This was the dynamic shared between me, my mom, and God. I could see the Father in the distance. I could hear His voice, and I appreciated being able to experience Him throughout my life. Yet I also craved the relationship with my mom. She in no way intentionally blocked my view. Rather, it was a mother's heart that held me across every situation.

Yet, here I stood, naked before God, with all of my frailties, cracks, and flaws on center stage. I was no longer a member of the audience peering into my own life experiences. I was on the stage with the curtain wide open for an audience of one—*Jesus Himself.* And He did not want me to do a performance of any kind. He simply wanted me to sit with Him, sit in my mess, and sit in His perfect, loving grace. God was up to something, and I felt the call to *do* something with all I had experienced with Him up to this point in my grief journey. *But for now, I needed to simply sit.*

###

March 8, 2014

9:30 a.m. I'm headed to the campus to work for a few hours before I head to San Diego later. Tomorrow morning, I'll be running in the San Diego Half Marathon, which I'm excited about. On my thirty-ninth birthday! So far it's been a low-key day. I received a birthday card from my coworkers, and a friend treated me to my favorite popcorn and organic juice. This week was rough, so I didn't really have a chance to fully appreciate the moments.

I'm content, but I'm feeling a bit down. The ninths of each month remind me of December 9th, the day Mama died. So I'm trying to simply focus on each moment and remain content, knowing that's what she would have wanted.

I have these existential moments at times when I feel incredibly alone—not separated from God, but disconnected from people on earth. Despite knowing more people now in California, I have a very limited *circle*. And I don't always feel like they always "get me." So today's March 8th, and that's what's happening in my world now. Content, yet down. Calm, yet antsy. Peaceful, yet frustrated.

It's a crazy tension that I've felt much more since Mama died. God is calling me to deepen my relationship with people.

March 8, 2014 revealed just what God was calling me to *do*. After sitting in, unpacking, and coming to grips with my emotional baggage for more than fifteen months at this point, God wanted me to create stronger relationships with those around me. My mom's death initiated my deepened relationship with Him, and now, He wanted me to exercise the intimacy I had learned with Him in other relationships. *I was overwhelmed and excited at the same time.*

My mom knew and understood me. Others closest to me, though in Texas, knew and understood me. God knew and understood me. Wasn't this enough? Even while asking myself the question, I knew the answer. No, this was not enough. God frequently reminded me of the cross—the vertical relationship with Him, which I had cultivated and grown to crave, and the horizontal relationship with other people. I had not, I must admit, devoted much time to developing strong bonds with those in California. My emotional walls remained high, yet I recognized the need to be more intentional in cultivating the relationships that I *did* have in California.

I began to intentionally reach out to a friend at work, as well as those within my church small group. Instead of canceling plans at the last minute, in an effort to steal away for emotional comfort, I forged ahead. It was uncomfortable and felt foreign. As I navigated these relationships, I had to resist the urge to listen as a psychologist to others' issues, despite this flowing so naturally. I had to resist the urge to participate from a distance, despite the fact that this was easier and well-received by others. I also had to fight my natural tendency to inwardly retreat, while at the same time exude an outward image. *This would require undoing years of learned impression management.*

Thankfully, my newfound relational efforts were met with open arms. Right outside of my emotional comfort zone, others were waiting to receive me, listen to me, and care for me. With my birthday only a day way, God had given me one of the greatest gifts—connection, through Him, with His children. This is what my mom had prayed for me prior to her death—greater intimacy with others. *It was incredibly beautiful and ironic that even in her death, she continued to give!*

> Right outside of my emotional comfort zone, others were waiting to receive me, listen to me, and care for me.

March 18, 2014

Holy crap! Bundy died today! Stanley called to tell me at the end of the workday. He told me that Bundy had been experiencing some back and leg pain and that he'd taken Bundy to the vet. The vet had prescribed steroids about two weeks ago. So anyway, Stanley said that over the past week, Bundy started experiencing more pain, as well as accidents, so Stanley took him back to the vet. He said that after blood work, the vet diagnosed Bundy with a dog version of MS. As far as treatments, the vet said there were really none. So the vet sent Bundy home today with pain meds. Stanley left Bundy at home today as usual and then returned home to Bundy unresponsive in his crate. Bundy was dead. Stanley said that the vet indicated that Bundy likely suffered a seizure and died in his crate sometime during the day.

Bundy's dead! I cried (and still am crying) about everything. In my mind, Bundy was the last physical connection to Mama. Now he's gone! I'm content that he's with Mama in heaven. She loved him and couldn't manage Bundy really being with anybody with her. She used to say, "Y'all don't like Bundy," then call his nickname, Bundy-B. He's with her now. That's some comfort.

I'm glad that Bundy's physical symptoms didn't show up until after Mama died. She wouldn't have been able to manage that, given her own fragile state. And I'm happy that I was able to spend an entire month with Bundy during my time home in December. He spent almost every night in the bed tucked away with me, Hunter, and Braxton. ☺ I was able to spend quality time with him and love on him for the first time ever. He looked so sweet and innocent, looking up at me in the bed each night. Bundy-B! I can say that I loved him, and I didn't think I'd be able to say that about his peanut head a few years ago.

So Mama's in heaven with all of her dogs—Baxter, Shiloh, and now Bundy. I hope she's happy now with her beagle babies.

I'm at a loss for words now. I'm going to pray and go to bed. Jesus, Jesus, Jesus!

I cannot say that I was one who held on to material items following my mom's death. In my mind, these things could not replace her, so I did not cling to them tightly. Nevertheless, her beagle, Bundy, was the most tangible, living thing (outside of my brother) connected to my mom at the time of her death. *And now, he was gone too.* On some level, I was overwhelmed at the reality of this truth. The news of Bundy's death shook me.

I had faced the death of my mom head-on, relaxing into the pain of it all. March 2014 marked the fifteen-month mark since her death, and I was *finally* getting my footing along my grief journey. The unpredictable and shaky ground that I had walked on since November 2012 finally felt more stable and dependable. *Then this!* Once again, there was no "ramp up" period, no time to prepare, no time to grieve in advance of his death, and no time to get settled into this new season of life. *Why did everything have to be so sudden?* I cannot imagine how my brother must have felt as he came home to a seemingly calm household, only to discover Bundy lying lifeless in his crate.

In the months following my mom's death, my brother cared for Bundy. After careful discussions about him, my brother and I made the decision for Bundy to remain in Texas, where things were more familiar. He had spent time at my brother's home, and my mom's scent was there. In addition, my brother had more space in his home for Bundy to explore, as well as interact with my brother's beagle. It just seemed like the right thing to do. Ironically, Bundy died in his home with his familiar belongings, just like my mom had.

Mixed with the shock of his untimely death, however, I also cherished the fact that Bundy was with his owner. My brother and I had joked that as much as our mom loved us, her children, she loved Bundy more! ☺ He offered constant companionship, which my mom craved even more following her strokes in spring 2012. I observed God's hand through it all, in spite of Bundy's sudden death. He had spared my mom from having to confront her own sickness, while at the same time focusing on Bundy's condition, which could have easily overwhelmed her. I know she would not have wanted her steady companion to suffer, *so perhaps, this too was a blessing masked by pain.*

> God was still in control, and with this sudden turn of events in my little family, I was reminded of His role as captain in my life even more!

God was still in control, and with this sudden turn of events in my little family, I was reminded of His role as captain in my life even more! Even with careful planning on my brother's and my part, we were not in control. It was now time to grieve Bundy's death, a familiar and known path, with God as captain and in total surrender.

###

March 23, 2014

Wow! This week was so bad that I didn't even have the energy or mind space to journal! Seriously! My week was spent taking in each frustrating breath and just trying to make it to the next moment. The load felt a little lighter on Thursday, following a conference I presented at. A woman came up to me after the presentation and thanked me for doing an excellent job. She called me an "angel." This was followed by my teaching my last Thursday night class, where a student shared that the class changed his life. I was literally speechless! God used the moments to remind me that He sees me, no matter where I am or how I feel.

For some reason, the issue of self-worth really affected me this week! The enemy was in my ear like a buzzing bee all week! OMG! I went from feeling unacknowledged at work to feeling unattractive to unworthy of love. It was a whirlwind! The week culminated in me going on an outing with a guy I met about a month ago. While we had a nice time out, our time together resulted in nothing more than a good-bye. So I left feeling like I wasn't good enough to even catch a guy's eye! Lord, I went through it last week!

Looking back at this journal entry, I sense the frustration I felt at the time. Yet, I can also sense the hope that God afforded me in the midst of it all. No matter where my mind traveled and no matter how deep my thoughts sunk, God cared. My mind screamed, "You are not worthy," and God used a student to let me know just how worthy I was. My mind screamed, "No one values what you do," and God used a woman in the audience of one of my presentations to let me know that my work mattered. I was making a difference. Even in my doubtful thoughts related to dating, God reminded me that I was beautiful in His eye.

I continued to grow in my understanding of God's nature and His character. As I increased my curiosity about who He was, He revealed more of Himself in sometimes subtle, yet profound, ways. *Rock bottom was the place where I met Jesus for the first time.* Rock bottom forced an inner exploration that culminated in my meeting the lover of my soul. Rock bottom forced me to look inward, and as I did, God's love flowed more freely.

> Rock bottom was the place where I met Jesus for the first time.

I had no idea where God was leading or how He would use me, but I was open and available ... *for the first time in my life!* This entire season had been about my connecting with the Father, thereby connecting with myself. I had walked into the fire, relaxed into the pain of everything, and exited the fire unscathed. The precise story of the three boys—Shadrach, Meschach, and Abednego—had been lived out in my life. In the midst of them holding on to God, in spite of the pain they anticipated, they met God and left the burning furnace without even a scratch or hint of smoke. "If it be so, our God whom we serve is able to deliver us from the furnace of blazing fire; and He will deliver us out of your hand, O king" (Daniel 3:17 NASB). *This was my testimony now.*

PART 5

Keep Walking into the Fire!

Mekel S. Harris, Ph.D.

April 7, 2014

Today was an *awesome* day! I slept in until 10:00 a.m., making it to work around 11:30 a.m. Then I had a brief meeting followed by an afternoon filled with finalizing loose ends. By the end of the workday (around 7:00 p.m.), I'd completed my manuscript proposal for my children's book! It's complete, and I'll be submitting the manuscript proposal to a publisher this week! And I truly believe this simple book has the potential to change the face of children's grief by providing a unique perspective of grief and loss. I'm excited, nervous, and ready at the same time!

The book was birthed on January 8, 2013, a random thought that I journaled about in one sitting. The words flowed with ease—only one month after Mama died. It's hard to believe that it's been almost exactly fifteen months since I initially wrote the book! Time has truly flown by! But here I am, more ready than ever. It's like time just opened up, and a space became available for me to work on the manuscript proposal. And just like the night that I wrote the book, in a matter of three short hours, the manuscript proposal was complete! Nothing but God!

Beauty for ashes, opportunity from heartache, and triumph in the midst of a trial—God is good, and I'm thrilled that He's using me in this way!

My testimony was coming to life right before my eyes!

> He has sent me to tell those who mourn that the time of the LORD's favor has come, and with it, the day of God's anger against their enemies. To all who mourn in

Israel, he will give a crown of beauty for ashes, a joyous blessing instead of mourning, festive praise instead of despair. In their righteousness, they will be like great oaks that the LORD has planted for his own glory. (Isaiah 61:2–3 NLT)

God's favor had undoubtedly arrived! For the first time since my mom's death, I felt like I was thriving in the midst of grieving, as opposed to merely surviving day to day. *He had transformed from a little tree to a great oak!*

Oak trees. A meditation on Isaiah 61:3 inspired me to research these types of trees, and what I discovered was so valuable and relevant to my experience. The oak tree has the capacity for growth for more than two hundred years and can thrive in a variety of habitats. Wood from the oak tree is commonly used to make flooring and furniture because of its sturdiness. Finally, the oak tree is known for its most distinctive quality, the acorn, a nutlike fruit. In a span of sixteen unpredictable months since my mom's death, God had strengthened and fashioned me into an oak tree via the emotional, physical, and emotional storms that I had encountered along my grief journey. I had begun the journey in shock and emotional stoicism, confronting my innermost parts with trepidation. Yet, through God's grace, I began to discover my capacity for growth and resilience across many situations and in April 2014, God revealed another fruit of my labor, a proposal. *It was my acorn, an identifiable product of all I had experienced in the preceding months.*

God's favor had been with me since the beginning of my grief journey. Just one month after my mom's death, the Lord planted a seed, in the form of words on a page and in my heart. On January 8, 2013, I was awakened in the middle of the night, after which I wrote in my journal. And sixteen months later, here I was submitting a proposal for a children's book! In the midst of my sadness, frustration, and anger, I had not appreciated the Lord's work in my life. I was not ready to embrace the fact that He could actually use my devastating circumstances for His glory and for my benefit. Yet here I was ... hopeful, optimistic, and grounded. It was a striking paradox of beauty and misery mixed together to strengthen my spiritual resolve and deepen my intimacy with the Father.

> It was a striking paradox of beauty and misery mixed together to strengthen my spiritual resolve and deepen my intimacy with the Father.

In order for there to be reconstruction, there must be destruction—the pearls of wisdom that God had shared with me in the months leading up to this point along my grief journey. I could finally see and appreciate the arc of the journey from devastation and shock to total chaos to understanding and blessing. I had always heard the phrase "beauty for ashes," but I did not fully comprehend what it meant until this moment. God had known all along what He planned to do in and through me as a result of my mom's death, as well as her life.

As I had felt at points along my journey, I believed that I had a sense of purpose for my grief. My mom's death had not been in vain, one of my greatest fears. *If I could do something to help others, I wanted to do so.* And the book was only one of the many opportunities that God would offer me so that I could do just that and help myself.

###

April 12, 2014

It's a little after 5:00 p.m., and I'm sitting in my car on a break at a children's camp. It's been a really good day. In our group meetings, several kids shared their stories, including the one assigned to me. I was really proud of her! I can't imagine facing the death of both my parents in such a horrific way. Yet she smiles. She laughs, and she moves forward with her young life. All of the kids here are amazing! The obstacles they've faced at such a young age are overwhelming! The kids inspire me each time I come to camp, and this experience is no different!

So ... Mama. I've thought of her often, and tears have welled up many times this weekend. I miss her *so* much! Someone shared that though this has been a difficult journey, he feels like a bolt now, strong, sturdy, and capable of building things. God has something for me to build right now, at this moment in my life. The children's book is one opportunity. My memoir is another. Each moment at camp is another. My life is not my own, and I must continue to build upon the foundation of strength that Mama laid so well. She wouldn't have it any other way. I know it. *"Move forward.* You are much stronger than you think, Miss Harris!" I can actually hear Mama telling me this. God, thank You for this day!

I can definitely see that I've healed since the last time I was at camp. I feel more present, even though my emotions continued to well up at different point throughout camp. It's OK. I'm OK. I know that this path God has me on is one with purpose. It's simply my job to allow the journey and recognize the doors and opportunities that God opens each day.

Lord, I pray that new doors might open, that You bless me with wisdom and favor, and that I touch many lives. I believe that You will do this, in Jesus's name!

I love you, Patricia Anne. *Always!*

Prior to April 2014, I was afraid to reenter the camp bubble as a volunteer because of the unpredictability of my emotions, as well as my fears that they would override my ability to care for the children entrusted to me. However, just one month prior to this point in time, I received a telephone call from one of the camp staff, inviting me to volunteer at the April camp. Despite my list of objections and Moses moments, she shared how my experiences throughout the grief journey mattered and had the potential to impact others' lives at camp.

It was a pivotal moment, a coupling of my increasing intimacy with God, those closest to me, and perhaps children whom I had never met. With tears in my eyes and a tickle in my throat, I shakily accepted the invitation to volunteer. *I knew in my heart that God was up to something!* God inspired me, yet again, to step beyond my comfort zone and exercise the intimacy I had grown to love with Him in my relationship with others.

Unlike other attempts to reveal my innermost thoughts and feelings regarding grief, I thought camp would be extraordinarily challenging. The nature of the camp centered on children sharing, as well as listening to painful stories of death and loss over a three-day period. At the same time, camp afforded children the opportunity to grow in resilience, as they observed others describe the grief journey and embraced new coping strategies of their own.

I observed children of all ages exhibit strength in the face of emotional weakness, joy in the face of pain. Within my small group, the visual image of a bolt, as well as the words used to describe it, heavily resonated within my spirit. *Strong. Sturdy. Capable.* This is how God saw me, and this is how He wanted me to see myself. My foundation had been shaken with my mom's death, and He had masterfully transformed me over time into a strong, sturdy, and capable woman! *I had the capacity to build something via my story!* In therapy, the idea of sharing my testimony was reinforced, as a means of offering me another strategy to manage my grief reactions.

> My foundation had been shaken with my mom's death, and He had masterfully transformed me over time into a strong, sturdy, and capable woman!

It was at this point along my grief journey where my passion for service united with my need to express myself in healthier ways. I recognized the futility in responding towards others in anger and frustration. I embraced the reality that sadness, in and of itself, was meaningless without intentionality. Camp solidified God's charge to me to live out my grief journey with purpose ... *for others, for myself, and ultimately, for His glory.*

###

May 1, 2014

It's a new month—May 1! Wow, this year has flown by! It's definitely been a busy one! Anyway, I'm sitting at a gate at LAX, preparing to travel to Boston to volunteer at a children's bereavement camp. I still can't believe that I was selected to serve across the country. *Crazy!* It was an open door that I chose to walk into with God's nudging. With each passing day, I'm becoming more fully aware that my calling in life is to inspire others in the area of grief and loss. I'm happy to note that every one of my professional activities this year fits with this theme. And my personal experiences have confirmed that this is the right path. I can't help but think of Mama. I know she would be proud. If it weren't for her, I wouldn't be doing any of this!

It's been remarkable to see how God has aligned all of my past experiences to get me to this point ... even using Mama's death in such an amazing way! It's a true fulfillment of Romans 8:28. Awesome!

Romans 8:28 (NIV) says, "And we know that in all things, God works for the good of those who love him, who have been called according to his purpose." As of May 2014, my life was a living embodiment of this Scripture. I could see God working everything out for my good, even in the midst of my lingering pain, as a result of my growing love for Him. Each one of my life experiences, including my mom's death, had been woven together to create the fabric of this new season of my life.

Just one month after reentering the camp bubble, I was en route to another out-of-state camp to serve yet again! In retrospect, I can see that God was wooing me, calling me unto Himself; and as He did, my love for Him grew more and more each day. I craved my alone time with Him, lamenting the moments when I was not able to devote myself to Him and His Word. *Intimacy.* God saw into me. I saw into me. Close friends saw into me. The children and staff at camp saw into me. My intimacy circle had finally expanded beyond my therapist and a few close family members.

> God was wooing me, calling me unto Himself; and as He did, my love for Him grew more and more each day.

This is what my mom had prayed for prior to her death. She longed for me to experience the power of deep and meaningful connections with others. I was heading to camp to do just that, and it was all because of her. Had I not experienced her death, I would not have been fully present—emotionally, physically, and spiritually—to serve others in a meaningful and intimate way. In opening myself up to intimacy with others, I afforded myself the gift of support, and others afforded me the gifts of acceptance and vulnerability.

God had walked alongside me all along, helping me chart a path for my good. From my own personal experience with my mom's death to camp to presentations targeting grief and loss, God orchestrated and connected each aspect of my life. It felt wonderful to be thought of in such a detailed and personal way! *God loved me! At this point, I was absolutely sure of that!*

###

May 3, 2014

Well, I'm back in the cabin. It's about 11:30 p.m., and it's been a long day. Tonight, the camp participated in a bonfire, a special time used to honor everyone's loved ones. The kids were remarkable in supporting one another in the midst of their sadness. It was the first time that my healing circle stayed after as a group to experience the bonfire together. I cried some, though I found myself smiling at the thought of Mama this time. It was like I now have a different vantage point, an appreciation of her death. In some strange way, it's like she needed to die in order for Stanley's and my relationship with the Lord to deepen. And her death has opened up so many opportunities to serve that I may not have had. I feel thankful!

In order for intimacy to fully blossom, one must feel supported. This is one of the nuggets I gained from the May 2014 camp experience. I observed young children with broken hearts demonstrate the capacity to support one another via words, body language, and explicit actions. I recognized the value of allowing others to support me in the same way outside of camp. God continued to expand my understanding of true intimacy in wonderful ways. As I began to trust the support around me, *relaxing into* the safe spaces God had provided since my mom's death, I felt more stable. My foundation continued to level out, and I regained my footing along the long and arduous grief journey.

> As I began to trust the support around me, relaxing into the safe havens God had provided since my mom's death, I felt more stable.

For the first time since my mom died, I was also stable enough to consider reasons for my mom's death without my emotions consuming me. Prior to this point in time, it was difficult for me to *fully* explore the spiritual reasons that my prayers for my mom's survival were not answered in the way that I had hoped. I had acknowledged the idolatry I engaged in with my mom, as well as God using her death to strengthen my relationship with Him. Yet I had never considered her death as an *open door* for other areas of my and my brother's life.

As I reflect upon this journal entry, I am struck again by the words of Romans 8:28, as well as Jeremiah 29:11. In all things, God *had* worked for my good, "for [He knew] the plans [He had] for [me], " … "plans to prosper [me] and not to harm [me], plans to give [me] hope and a future." Before the foundation of the world, God knew that my mom would die on December 9, 2012. He knew the plans He had for me, *in the midst of my grief.* He knew that His plans would not harm me, but would give me a hope and a future. *He knew!*

And just like that, I realized that the anger and frustration I had previously embraced was gone. What was there to be angry and frustrated about? My mom was no longer experiencing pain and discomfort. *He promised that He would not harm me.* Seventeen months into the grief journey, I was emotionally, physically, and spiritually stable. *He promised that He would give me hope.* Doors had opened for me to share my grief journey, as well as support others who were grieving. *He promised that He would give me a future.* God had, indeed, honored His Word!

###

Mekel S. Harris, Ph.D.

May 10, 2014

So it's almost 11:00 p.m. now. Tomorrow is Mother's Day, and I've been thinking about Mama a lot, obviously. I think about her all the time! I can only imagine what she's doing now. I know she's with the Lord in heaven. It must be so beautiful and calm where she is. No more problems, no more pain, no fear. Only peace, love, and complete harmony. And God! It makes me wonder what it's like to be fully in His presence, to see His face! I want to see Him!

May 2014 marked the second Mother's Day that I would not physically be with my mom. She had always disliked Mother's Day, as it forced mothers to consider their evolving roles, children to lament the death of their mothers, and women to question their ability to bear children of their own. I had certainly experienced the things my mom noted throughout my adult life as a single and unmarried woman. Yet on this day, I simply reflected on how comfortable and at peace my mom was with God. I recalled many sweet memories she and I shared throughout my life, as well as her boisterous laugh and smile.

This was in stark contrast to the way I had experienced my first Mother's Day without her. At that time, I flew to Texas to physically be with my brother, the only other person who could understand the grief experience as my mom's child. We visited her crematorium wall and talked with one another about precious moments with our mom. After that, we ate at a local restaurant and returned to my brother's home, where I slept in the very bed that my mom had died in. Needless to say, it was a challenging experience for me, which triggered so many thoughts and emotions surrounding my mom's death.

By May 2014, however, I had resolved the fact that my mom's crematorium was only a warehouse for her ashes. *She was not there.* I had reconciled the fact that moving to Texas to "be with her" was not necessary since she was with the Lord. I did not travel to Texas for Mother's Day, as I had the year before. Instead of mourning her absence, I celebrated her presence across so many situations in my life. Indeed, she had been *present* for so much! I cannot think of one situation or decision that she was not a part of, actually.

> I had resolved the fact that my mom's crematorium was only a warehouse for her ashes. *She was not there.*

I also began to wonder more about life after physical death, focusing on eternal things. "So we fix our eyes not on what is seen, but on what is unseen, since what is seen is temporary, but what is unseen is eternal" (2 Corinthians 4:18 NIV). My mom's life was temporary, and I knew in my spirit that God did not want me to dwell on what I could see—the cemetery and her crematorium. Rather, He challenged me to focus on the unseen realm, where He dwelled, where my mom was, and where I would be someday. This helped me place her death in perspective, against the backdrop of my Christian faith. The cliché "life is short" rang true, and I longed to center my heart on those things yet to come in eternity.

Typical of God and my relationship with Him, the transition from deep sorrow to joy felt sudden. Yet, I know that He had been methodical in helping me sort through everything within myself to help me arrive at this point along my grief journey. As I drew near to Him in my grief, God afforded me glimpses of His face. *I* was hungry for so much more! I believe that the Father encouraged me to fervently seek Him like never before, for in my pursuit, I would see Him face-to-face.

###

June 1, 2014

Church was wonderful as usual. The pastor preached from the book of Job, and a family shared about their journey of adoption. The bottom line was about embracing the will of God above all else, trusting His heart, even when you can't necessarily see His hand. Not praying for things you don't want but embracing whatever may come along life's journey. I couldn't help but think of Mama's death, an event that I never would have wanted to face. The timing of it, the pace surrounding it—it all came out of nowhere, totally unexpected. Then within a month, she was gone in the blink of an eye.

So I get Job's loss on some level—the sadness, anger, and confusion of it all. Yet so much has come from Mama's death. My relationship with the Lord has deepened. My understanding of who I am as a woman has grown. God was up to something all along. I still don't fully understand the journey God has me on. But I sit here at peace, aimless and open to whatever God has, whichever *turn* I'll take next.

Throughout life, a complex paradox often arises—one that forces us to wrestle with joy in the midst of suffering, clarity in the midst of life's fogs, and peace in the midst of chaos and confusion. I had finally reached the place where I was able to hold opposing truths about my mom's death in one hand. Was her death sudden and devastating? *Yes!* Did her death catapult me into a tailspin for many months, resulting in emotional, physical, and spiritual disarray? *Yes!* Had I experienced the lowest emotional depths of my life as a result of her death? *Yes!*

At the same time, had I discovered intimacy with God and others as a result of my mom's death? *Yes!* Did I have a better appreciation of myself following her death? *Yes!* Was I more spiritually attuned and grounded than I had ever been before her death? *Yes!* The answer to every question I posed to myself and God was unequivocally yes. *How can that be?* I wondered. In my quest to understand life's many paradoxes, I stumbled upon an article that described life as a ball of gray yarn. In life, we have extreme moments, ups and downs that guide and shape us. Each of us is comfortable in the extremes because we either have no need for God or wholly depend on Him for every breath. It is life lived at the extremes!

Of course, God is with us in the extremes of life—the births of babies, the deaths of loved ones, marriages, and divorces. Nevertheless, the majority of life is not lived at one extreme or another. It is lived in the gray zone. Throughout the eighteen months along my grief journey, my life had been lived in shades of gray. I experienced extreme moments, yes, but the majority of the months following my mom's death were gray. These were what I describe as the "messy months"—the months when I could not easily default to any particular emotional, physical, or spiritual stance.

> I came to the conclusion that solely living in life's extremes is the easy way to live. It is the messiness, the gray zone, which requires great faith and persistence.

I came to the conclusion that solely living in life's easy way to live. It is the messiness, *the gray zone*, which requires great faith and stamina. It is in the gray space where we can neither see far in the distance ahead nor in the past. It is that chasm between embracing new spiritual heights and reflecting upon weighty spiritual lows. Gray is the place where the flames of pain join with the comforts of peace. For me, God dwelled in the gray zone.

It was His intent for me to stumble upon my cracks, flaws, insecurities, and broken pieces. It was His will for me to confront them and pursue Him, all for the purpose of spiritual and emotional rebuilding. It was His perfect and uniquely design for me to be comfortable being seen for who I truly was. It was His—my life, my mom's life, my brokenness, and my healing. *It was all His!—*

###

July 13, 2014

It's about 9:30 a.m., and I'm getting ready for church. I thought I'd stop and journal for a minute because I had a dream about Mama. Apparently, she was not feeling well, so I went with her to the doctor. While there, Mama was having a hard time remembering something, and when the doctor came to chat with her, he said that she had early dementia as part of Alzheimer's disease. We left

Relaxing Into the Pain

the doctor's office, and in the next scene of the dream, Mama was taking a bath. For some reason, she was very weak and couldn't hold her torso or head up in the bathtub. At moments, she'd sink beneath the bathwater, and I'd run over to help her up. I finally found a long and sturdy pillow, which I placed in the water to help prop her up. And that was the end of the dream. *Crazy!* Nineteen months, and this is the dream I have.

This was only the second time I had seen my mom since her death. I had continued to pray that God would allow me to peer into her experience in some way, without much success in the preceding months. But on July 13, 2014, she was there. However, this was not the type of interaction I anticipated via my dreams. As a psychologist, I attempted to explore themes within the dream in order to interpret what I thought it represented. I concluded, in the end, that God offered me a glimpse into what may have been if my mom had actually survived the cancer.

One of my mom's biggest fears was developing dementia and/or Alzheimer's disease because of her own mother's diagnosis and the challenges my mom faced trying to offer care for my grandmother in the midst of her disease. At least monthly, my mom spoke with my brother and me about never wanting to be a burden in her old age. Of course, we assured her that this would not be the case; however, she insisted nonetheless. My mom prided herself on being independent and capable of making her own decisions about every aspect of her life. So living with Alzheimer's disease, unaware of the things and people dearest to her, would have been emotionally devastating.

In the preceding months, as my relationship with God grew, I began to look to Him as a loving Father, again reflecting on Jeremiah 29:11. He promised that He would never harm me, as no good father would. From my viewpoint, this dream was an example of God sparing me from a future filled with much more sadness and decline than my mom's death had been. The thought of bearing the weight of my ailing mother's deterioration over a longer period of time, coupled with a worsening mental condition, was overwhelming to me. I believed that God spared my brother and me from this and instead, offered her an opportunity to die with her dignity intact. Up until the last day that my mom spoke, she knew who she was. She knew who my brother and I were, and she knew where she was. She was mentally intact, consistent with the way she had lived throughout her sixty-three years on earth. *God had spared me from harm, indeed!*

> He promised that He would never harm me, as no good father would.

###

August 24, 2014

It's about 5:00 p.m. here in Tallinn, and I'm sitting atop what I believe is one of the pinnacles of the city, a beautiful cemetery/memorial area near Pirita. What a beautiful place! I decided to leave the hotel around 3:00 p.m., after sleeping for most of the day, and venture out on foot. I hopped on a bus for about two miles and then got off near Kadrioru Park. I was instantly mesmerized and decided to walk along the beach and harbor line (Pirita Tee) for a while. It was definitely worth the walk!

Relaxing Into the Pain

I'm looking at a beautiful sculpture that comes out of the ground now—a pair of hands. It looks like they are hands held up in surrender as unto the Lord. Beautiful! I love how my thoughts are never far from the Lord! No matter where I go, I constantly think about Him and reflect upon His goodness, especially in light of everything I've been through since Mama died.

By the end of summer 2014, I felt like a completely different person, in terms of how I understood and related to God. I had traveled all around the world, encountering God in new and wonderful ways. It was as if the Lord wanted me to experience certain things along my grief journey, as a reminder of my relationship with Him. In the preceding months, I had traveled to India, where I observed a physical manifestation of surrender. Now in Estonia, I had stumbled upon a pair of hands that reinforced God's messages to me throughout the journey. *Relax into the pain. Surrender your whole being to Me. Allow Me to be your captain, once and for all.*

I continued to experience God as Father, and He continually provided for me, His child. As I yielded to His ways, I felt closer to Him. *Surrender.*

If you set your heart right, and put out your hands to Him, and if you put away the sin that is in your hand, do not let wrongdoing be in your tents. Then, you will be able to lift up your face without sin. You would be strong and not afraid. For you would forget your trouble, remembering it as waters that have passed by. Your life would be brighter than noon. Darkness would be like the morning. Then you would trust, because there is hope. You would look around and rest and be safe. (Job 11:13–18 CEV)

God wanted more from me, however, despite me stretching out my hands to Him. It was time for yet *another* change in direction along my grief journey. God was calling me even closer to Him, and this required me to dig even deeper into myself and confront hidden sins. *How could I simultaneously hold Him and wrongdoing in my hands?* One needed to be released in order to fully worship God. I was forced to file through my mental rolodex and identify additional areas that needed God's light.

Anger … *check*. Pride … *check*. Unforgiveness … *check*. Selfishness … *check*. Lust … *check*. And the list went on and on. *It was as if God were unsettling my solid foundation yet again!*

> God wanted more from me, however, despite my putting out my hands to Him. It was time for yet *another* change in direction along my grief journey.

I found myself frustrated, yet faithful, to the Lord at this point along my journey. I wondered why God would not simply allow me to enjoy the stability that had returned after so many months of my feeling emotionally, physically, and spiritually unsteady. I was still healing from my mom's death, attempting to embrace the devastation of it all. How could God not understand this? *Then it dawned on me!* My relationship with God, which was similar to other relationships, was constantly evolving. God had extended His grace toward me as I settled into a deeper intimacy with Him since my mom's death. At the same time, He challenged me to further grow into the woman of God He created me to be. Though I wanted my mom's death, as well as my healing thus far, to shield me from more spiritual stretching, God was not in agreement. *Oh, there was much more growing up for me to do on the horizon!* "For the LORD corrects those he loves, just as a father corrects a child in whom he delights" (Proverbs 3:12 NLT).

November 23, 2014

"Peace will come when you embrace the task for which you were created." My dad and I are en route to Beijing, China at the moment, and I stumbled across this quote written on a piece of paper stuffed in the seatback pocket. God is always trying to tell me something, and I think I know just what He's referring to.

Throughout the fall 2014, I continued to wrestle with God's charge to stretch, although I knew that this is what was required of me to grow in intimacy with God and others. It was a time filled with restless nights, in part because of my occasional insomnia. (Yes, nearly two years after my mom's death, I still struggled to sleep throughout the night.) I was also restless because of God's whispers to unearth additional areas in my life that needed to be exposed.

In therapy, Amy and I continued to focus on my grief journey, with emphasis on strategies for exploring meaning along the way. We agreed just prior to November 2014 that I had reached the end of our time together, which I simultaneously embraced and rejected. Amy had been my practice ground for intimacy beyond my relationship with God, and with her and God's help, I had extended my intimacy circle to a few close friends and family. But God's newest plan for me to stretch even further in my relationship with Him involved only Him and me. It was as if He had observed my steps in the right direction, in terms of intimacy and saw fit to add an additional layer of challenge. It was time to step even further into the uncharted parts of myself–for better or worse.

> Peace will come when you embrace the task for which you were created.

I found it befitting of God for me to find a random slip of paper on a plane from California to China. *Of all places!* The words on the paper penetrated my spirit. "Peace will come when you embrace the task for which you were created." I envisioned the task as one that would require additional self-exploration and exposure, the epitome of vulnerability and intimacy. It was yet *another* paradox—the more I allowed others to experience the fullness of who I was, the more peace I would achieve in my life. Admittedly, I had wrestled with the hidden parts of myself for far too long. *Despite the fact that I was nervous, I was also ready.*

###

December 11, 2014

So I survived another twenty-one-hour road trip from California to Texas yesterday! I arrived safely at Stanley's house around 3:30 a.m. this morning. It was nice to be greeted with hugs and smiles! I slept until 8:30 a.m., stayed up for a couple of hours, and then dozed off again at 2:30 p.m. And I've been up ever since! Overall, I feel great! I'm a little stiff from the car ride, but I'm good! Anyway, when Stanley got home, we decorated our Christmas tree and sang along to the radio. It was nice! I realized that we didn't really celebrate Christmas fully last year. Mama would have been happy tonight.

Christmas 2011 was my brother's and my last Christmas with my mom. Oh, the sweet memories and good times we had! My brother had several Wii games, one of which was bowling. So my mom took to the lanes and bowled her way to victory in my brother's living room! R & B songs blasted from the radio, and my mom, who loved to sing, sang her heart out as my brother and I looked on. She even danced with all of our beagles around the Christmas tree!

Creating new memories with my brother in December 2014 was absolutely wonderful! My brother had strategically purchased purple lights and ornaments to honor my mom's fight with pancreatic cancer. We sang along to one of her favorite radio stations, taking special note of her favorite artists and songs. It was as if she were right there with us, dancing and singing along. This was the essence of what Amy and I had discussed for so many months in therapy. Finding ways to memorialize and honor my mom's life gave me purpose and helped place my grief in perspective. My mom's spirit was still alive in my brother and me, and for that, I was incredibly thankful!

> Finding ways to memorialize and honor my mom's life gave me purpose and helped keep my grief in perspective.

After finishing the Christmas tree and enjoying dinner, my brother and I then traveled to our extended family's home to enjoy more Christmas festivities. *It was a blessed holiday, one that sparked the beginning of new traditions for me and my brother!*

###

February 20, 2015

"God will only give you the promise if you go through the process." I'm watching a pastor preach online, taking notes and listening to an awesome message! *God, are You speaking to me again?* Yes, I know I've been a bit slack on sharing my testimonies throughout the past month or so, but it's been a busy season. It's hard to believe that I had surgery one month ago! And I'll be returning to work soon after several weeks of recovery. Anyway, it feels like every part of me is going through a process of some sort. *Can I just rest for a little while?*

After receiving a word from God to dig even deeper spiritually, I had not done much to that end in the New Year. First, I had undergone major surgery in January 2015, leaving me focused on physical recovery. In early February 2015, I had begun creating a new private practice space, which required mental energy and focus. This did not leave much room for self-analysis. Nevertheless, these were mere excuses in God's eye. *By the end of February 2015, God was still summoning me deeper into His presence.*

In November 2014, it had been a message on a slip of paper. And now, it was a message from an online pastor. *I would say that God was employing every tactic to gain my attention!* He was, indeed, speaking to me again. The more I thought about it, the more I tried to dissect the process God had *already* taken me through. Again, I reflected on the cross. Following my mom's death, God had deepened my vertical relationship with Him via delving into my inner hurts and pain. As God observed that my relationship with Him was growing, He then launched me into the horizontal aspect of my spiritual life via relationships with others. This was followed by my retreating from a major relationship with my therapist and even stronger pursuit of God. Now, God wanted me to further expand my understanding via shedding myself of prior sins that I had carried over the years.

Logically and spiritually, I understood it. Emotionally, I was tired. Yet, I forged forward, trusting that God would honor the message on the slip of paper and offer me peace. "No one puts a piece of unshrunk cloth on an old garment, for the patch tears away from the garment, and a worse tear is made. Neither is new wine put into old wineskins. If it is, the skins burst and the wine is spilled and the skins are destroyed. But, new wine is put into fresh wineskins, and so both are preserved" (Matthew 9:16–17 ESV).

> I forged forward, trusting that God would honor the message on the slip of paper and offer me peace.

Within the next few weeks after this journal entry, I took a step of faith in the presence of God and my small church group. I had received the new wine offered by God through His amazing grace, and I chose to remove the old wineskins so His wine could flow freely in and through me. My vulnerability before man was met with pure compassion, understanding, and grace. This was the beginning of the process, and even then, I knew that God had kept His promise! *Oh, what an awesome Father He is!*

###

April 2, 2015

It's about 12:30 p.m., and I'm sitting in a Subway, eating lunch across the street from the Hawaii Convention Center. Today's devotion says, "Only God's grace could reach so low and lift so high." It gave me pause to consider this current space. God reached so low into my darkest moments, sadness, and grief the last time I was in Honolulu in 2013 (a year and half ago). Yet here I am, and God has lifted me so high! I'm here again, presenting at an international training summit by invitation, residing in a hotel room on the thirty-five floor with an ocean view, and I sat atop a mountain looking down over Honolulu just a couple of days ago! Wow! *Tears.*

April 2, 2015 was my "full circle" moment along my grief journey. It certainly was not the end, as grief requires lifelong travel. However, it reflected the arc of God's "full circle" revelations within my heart. Things finally made sense, especially after crossing over the threshold out of hiding and into openness. I began my fire walk in August 2013 in Honolulu, the very place I was in April 2015. After experiencing the lowest point along my grief journey, God had catapulted me into a new season of faith, trust, and intimacy with Him. He had wooed me endlessly while in Hawaii, seducing me with beautiful sunsets, clear waters, and rainbows.

It seemed fitting for Him to make Himself known, yet again, against this amazing and memorable backdrop. *Only God's grace could reach so low and lift so high! It astounded me!* God's grace had reached into the darkest parts of me in this same place almost two years earlier. God's grace had also lifted me so high in this very moment! I literally sobbed as I considered all that God had done in and through me in a relatively short amount of time. I sobbed because I finally appreciated the *process* that God had taken me through over the past two and a half years since my mom's death. I sobbed because for the first time, I embraced *all of me* without judgment.

> I literally sobbed as I considered all that God had done in and through me in a relatively short amount of time. I sobbed because I finally appreciated the *process* that God had taken me through over the past two and a half years since my mom's death.

I had walked in the valley of the shadow of death, and God was with me. I had stepped into the fire yet exited without a hint of smoke or any other residue. I had walked out into the ocean with my eyes fixed on Jesus, and He kept me lifted. I had sunk into the deepest pit, and He raised me up to level ground. Instead of needing to be lifted up this time, however, I sat atop a mountain and peered out over the beautiful city of Honolulu! It was a literal and metaphorical manifestation of God's love and grace. *Only God could do that!*

My experience in April 2015 epitomized the fullness of God's character. Not only was He my loving Father, but He was also the lover of my soul. He cared for me so tenderly along the grief journey, yet He challenged me to stretch in ways that benefited me and others. He replaced my old wineskins so that I could receive the fresh wine He offered at this point in my life. God afforded me intimacy, the gift that my mom had always desired for me, and in doing so, I received the greatest blessings in relationship to myself and with others. He loved His child, and I loved Him with every fiber of my being!

To God be the glory for all that He has done! Amen!

ADDITIONAL REFLECTIONS

I have always appreciated the beauty of self-reflection and enjoy the opportunities to review my thoughts and personal growth over time. To this end, I offer a few final thoughts about my grief journey thus far.

God uniquely designed my journey, paying careful attention to what I needed along the way. At moments, I questioned the suddenness of my experiences—my mom's diagnosis, hospice, her death, life events following her death. I came to the conclusion that what I perceived as God's constant shifts were expressions of His love. Would a loving father allow his child to remain stuck in quicksand? *Of course not!* From the moment my mom died, God recognized the ease with which I could have remained stuck—immobilized by my feelings—throughout my grief journey.

As I look back over the arc of my journey to date, I see pivotal junctures when God jolted me out of my emotional quicksand. The first juncture was my return to California from Texas in January 2013. Quicksand had the potential to lock my heels into place at that time, and God provided a way of escape via a twenty-four-hour trek across the country. Remaining in my mom's home and staying wedded to her physical belongings would have

done more harm than good to me. So God shifted the tides and evoked full-throttle action in co-managing my mom's affairs and returning to my normal routine.

Relief came in April 2013 with one telephone call, as I began individual therapy. Week after week, God used my therapist to challenge beliefs, develop healthier coping strategies, and increase my self-awareness. He never allowed me to get comfortable throughout the process. Rather, God's voice consistently reigned through my therapist's mouth, and I wrestled to explore parts of me that I had never known prior to my mom's death.

In May 2013, I boarded the nearly uninhabited plane in route to Maryland. I had spent nearly six months at that point functioning in autopilot, completely disengaged from my heartache and pain. The Lord used a solitary and peaceful space for me to feel safe enough to pour out my pain in His presence. From the airplane to the hotel, God carried me and again, pulled me from the tightening grips of depression. He caused me to ponder the life of David and provided me with enough strength to encourage myself in the midst of darkness. Then God offered raindrops (what I perceived as His tears) to remind me that while my spirit felt dead, I was very much alive.

August 2013 offered another critical juncture along my grief journey. I had recognized the life within me in prior months, opening up a space in my heart to actually receive God. In Hawaii, He wooed me at every turn, affording me a glimpse into His role as a loving father, the lover of my soul, my friend, and a lifelong journeyman through every trial that I might face. Just as I embraced Him as such, He shifted the tides yet again, calling me to a foreign altar to cry out to Him and connect with others. *Intimacy became the theme of the season.*

From September through November 2013, the Lord lovingly challenged me to enter new spaces in relationships and put what I had learned in therapy to the test. My test manifested itself in the form of a big red door, one that I anxiously entered and confidently exited. Then in February 2014, He provided a living example of what surrender looked like, again shifting me into a space to exercise my faith and relationship with Him, as well as with others.

Then a walking trip around the city of Tallinn in Estonia in August 2014 prompted yet another change in direction. God used a beautiful sculpture to remind me of the need to not only surrender my pain, but also my sin to Him. My outstretched hands could no longer balance the weight of grief and sin at the same time. In this season, the Father challenged me to explore the root of my struggles with intimacy in ways I had never explored. He used discomfort, yet again, to help me wrestle my way out of the quicksand that threatened to consume me and keep me distant from the love I so desperately needed from Him and others.

God loves order and closure, so it comes as no surprise to me that He allowed me to travel back to the place where He pursued and showered me with affection. April 2015 represented a full circle moment in Hawaii, a literal manifestation of the Father's ability to carry me out of my darkest pit and lift me up to the highest peak. Though my journey is lifelong and unpredictable still, awareness of what God has done in (almost) three years brings me great joy and hope. *Oh, He has loved me well, indeed!* I would be in a much different emotional, physical, and spiritual place had it not been for His enduring love and amazing grace!

###

Here are a few final thoughts about my warrior, Patricia Anne Harris.

Now where do I begin? Psychoanalytic theorists within the field of psychology assert the importance of exploring one's childhood, particularly early childhood relationships, as a means of understanding one's overt and intrapsychic motives throughout one's life. While a debate regarding the efficacy of such theorists' claims is beyond the scope of this book, I will say that it makes sense for my story. In particular, the relationship developed with my mother was very substantial and memorable. You see, my earliest recollections of my mother include her pressing my hair at the stove, a common phenomenon between African-American mothers and daughters, as well as her driving me to a select magnet school roughly forty miles from our family home each morning before going to work herself. I vividly recall my mother preparing lectures for her students, leaving no stone unturned, with regard to her handouts or projector slides. From a much earlier time in my life, I recall my mother attempting to dry the tears from her eyes following a marital dispute and doing everything in her power to shield my brother and me from adult conversations, even at her own expense.

Patricia Anne Harris was a warrior in my eye, a woman who, regardless of the situation, stood her ground, spoke up for herself, and rallied until the bitter end. I observed her engage in this way throughout her career as a nurse and nursing instructor, in her rocky marriage to my father, within her personal friendships, and throughout her relationship with me and my brother. She was a strong woman, no doubt! And my relationship with her centered, in large part, on her strength. See, I was referred to as the "sensitive" child, a description that I loathed growing up but one I have begun to embrace as an adult. I was the youngest child in the household, the child who delighted in attention and affection from others, the child who felt emotionally unwell when tensions grew high or when conversations grew intense within the home. I cried easily, even when my bed was not made to perfection or when someone looked at me "the wrong way." One particular memory comes to mind here. My grandmother visited our family one summer, and she slept with me in my bed throughout her stay. One night, I awoke in the middle of the night. I was unable to return to sleep, so I tried to wake my grandmother. Rather than getting up as I had anticipated, my grandmother snored even more loudly next to me, unfazed by my futile attempts to wake her. For some reason, I felt abandoned by her actions, and instantly, my feelings were hurt. I sat on the edge of the bed and cried that night … for no apparent reason at all. Yes, I was *that* child.

My mother, on the other hand, was not *that* mother. While she was definitely responsive to my physical and emotional needs, her tolerance for crying and things of that sort was limited. I often heard, "Stop crying, Mickey (my nickname)!" or "What are you crying about now, girl?" out of her mouth. In most cases, what resulted were more tears on my part, based upon my sensitivity to constructive criticism of any sort. I realize now that her inquiry was an attempt to strengthen my resolve and prepare me for the real scrutiny she knew I would receive from others throughout my life. However, as a child, when life would throw its curveballs (in the form of petty friendships, miscommunications, etc.), my tendency was to steal away, cry for a spell, and then seek help from my warrior.

She was incredibly skilled at serving in this capacity! It was as if one of her purposes in life was to fight my battles, along with hers. I mean, she really deserved an award of some sort for her abilities.

A plaque to hang on the wall, a medal to wear around her neck, something to reflect her talent! In high school, another student called me a name that was not my first name, which resulted in my getting into a physical altercation. Was I concerned? No. After detention that day, I went home and told my mother the entire story, and she scheduled a meeting the very next morning with the school principal. And while I have no idea what she told the principal, I remember getting dressed the next morning, heading to school, and carrying on with my day as if the day before never happened. Voila, the *mess* was cleaned up! On another occasion, a school counselor informed me that I, a straight-A honor roll student, would be better suited for the military after high school. And again, my mother visited with him. Then after shopping for a new outfit with my mother, I was honored at a scholarship banquet, where I received an academic scholarship from a prestigious private institution!

Warrior—that was her name in my book. Oh, did I mention that she also fought other, more personal battles outside of the ones fought on my behalf? In my childish mind's eye, her primary battlefield was her marriage. Through twists, turns, ups, and downs, my mother experienced several valleys as a wife. In addition, she faced several physical battles in her sixty-three-year journey. From Crohn's disease to a hysterectomy to high blood pressure and strokes to cancer, she was a warrior. She battled each physical disease while working full-time in some capacity. My brother and I joke that she was the only person who could literally experience several mini strokes while driving (probably with one hand), drive herself to the emergency room, and call us during her physical exam! In 2007, I remember racing across town from school after receiving an emergency call from the hospital, indicating that my mother had suffered several strokes. Somehow, after driving more than ninety miles per hour to the hospital, I jumped out of the car and dashed into the emergency room only to find my mother laughing with a medical technician on the edge of a gurney! *At that point I was the one who needed a blood pressure cuff placed on my arm!* On a second emergency occasion, my brother's journey to the emergency room was similar, only this time my mother was packing her bags to head home by the time he arrived! I had not even arrived, and she was being discharged with all things "within normal limits!" *That is just the type of warrior she was!*

Now we all know that even warriors need some downtime, right? *Wrong!* My mother's *recovery* periods were typically filled with her sleeping for a day, followed by a return to work or return to solving others' (okay, my) problems. In retrospect, it was quite easy for both of us to fall into our old patterns of communicating and solving life's issues. My mother was known for being inquisitive (well, actually nosy), so she really enjoyed being *in the mix* with regard to my brother's and my personal affairs. And of course, one of her most favorite topics to discuss with me was dating. If anything could spark physical healing on her part, boys, dates, telephone conversations, or any related matters most certainly could! *And the discussion flowed ... and flowed ... and flowed ... often for hours on end!* From my first thoughts of dating to my first official date in eleventh grade, my mother charted the course, paved the way, and steered me through the process ... gladly and without hesitation. *She was, indeed, a warrior!*

FINAL THOUGHTS AND PRAYER

It has been an overwhelming, yet beautiful, journey thus far. Through it all, my love for Christ has deepened, and my trust in Him has strengthened. My love for myself has also widened, affording space for intimacy in ways I could never have imagined. I have learned to relax into the pain of my grief, as well as journey into areas beyond its reach. *How deep the Father's love is for me ... and you!* I pray that as you reflect on your own journey, God's love is apparent, even in moments of heartache and darkness. God bless you, my brothers and sisters in Christ, for traveling alongside me over the course of many pages!

Prayer

Father, may those reading this book grow in the knowledge that You and You alone are their warrior—a warrior who will stand firm on the battlefield when they lack strength. Allow each man, woman, and child to experience you as Abba (Daddy), as they yield their heartache, pain, and sadness into your loving arms.

Father, carry them in the hard moments, as they relax into the pain of their experience. May my brothers and sisters be open to healing, wholeness, and transformation in the sacred space of grief. Amen ... and amen!

Made in the USA
Lexington, KY
02 July 2016